*Also by Deborah J. Levine:*

*The Matrix Model Management System:
Guide to Cross Cultural Wisdom*

*Inspire Your Inner Global Leader:
True Stories for New Leaders*

*Teaching Christian Children about Judaism*

*Religious Diversity in our Schools*

# GOING SOUTHERN:

# The No-Mess Guide to Success in the South

## By Deborah J. Levine

*GOING SOUTHERN: The No-Mess Guide to Success in the South*
© Deborah Levine 2013
By Deborah J. Levine
Published by Deborah Levine Enterprises, LLC
Chattanooga, TN 37412
1 (888) 451-2798


**web:** www.deborahlevine.com

**e-mail:** info@deborahlevine.com

# FOREWORD

Growing up in the Appalachian hills of east Tennessee during the 1940s and 1950s, I did not realize that I was part of a distinct "culture." My opportunities to travel widely, first in the United States and then around the world, revealed to me the many behaviors, dialects, and artifacts that defined my culture of origin. So, it often takes moving outside of one's parochial setting to see and be able to describe to others what it is like.

This fun and highly useful book is the result of Deborah J. Levine's ability to view aspects of Southern culture through more objective eyes and with the benefit of her keen insights as a relative newcomer. Ms. Levine's own family history and background prepared her to view her adopted Southern culture with appreciation for its rich idiosyncrasies, its ancient roots, and its importance to the success of travelers and immigrants from other parts of the world. Her insights are warm and vital because she delivers them in an engaging storytelling style that is itself an example of Southern literary culture.

*Going Southern: The No-Mess Guide to the South* will be an entertaining as well as practical introduction to my native region for anyone who wants to live, work, play, and learn in a part of the world that has proved endlessly fascinating to the centuries of natives and visitors with the good fortune to call it home.


Dr. Roger G. Brown
Chancellor Emeritus
University of Tennessee at Chattanooga

# TABLE OF CONTENTS

**PART I: WHERE & WHEN** ...................................................................7
  **Chapter 1:** *The Introduction: Why Take This Journey?* .........7
  **Chapter 2:** *The Decision: Going Southern, Y'all* ..............11
  **Chapter 3:** *The Intersection: Where Geography & History Connect* ...24
  **Chapter 4:** *The Names: Why Native American History Is Relevant Today* ....................................................................36
  **Chapter 5:** *The Myths: How to Navigate the Old South and Avoid Missteps* ..................................................................45
  **Chapter 6:** *The Choo Choo Factor: How Terminus Was Terminated & Reborn-ish* ................................................................55

**PART II: WHO & WHAT** ...................................................................68
  **Chapter 7:** *The Race Issue: What Outsiders Should Know* .................69
  **Chapter 8:** *The Traditionalists: Who Are the Real Southerners?* .........85
  **Chapter 9:** *The Faithful* ..................................................99
  **Chapter 10:** *The Icons: Who's Trending & Why You Should Follow* ........116
  **Chapter 11:** *The Big Picture Folks; What New Southerners Bring to the Table* .......................................................................128

**PART III: WHY & HOW** ...................................................................141
  **Chapter 12:** *The Social Scene: How to Be Sociable, No Matter What* ......142
  **Chapter 13:** *The Southernisms: What the Colorful Sayings of the South Really Say* ...........................................................157
  **Chapter 14:** *The Performance: Why It's Always Time for Your Close-Up* ....166
  **Chapter 15:** *The Relationship: How Are You Fixin' to Fix It?* ..........175
  **Chapter 16:** *The Secret Ingredient: Why Storytelling is the Key* .......185

# PART I: WHERE & WHEN

## Chapter 1: *The Introduction: Why Take This Journey?*

The U.S. Southeast is undergoing an economic transformation with an impact as great as the Civil War and the Civil Rights Movement. This book is a guide to the culture that is emerging where Global and Southern now connect. The pace of globalization in the South has increased every year, but the last half dozen years have been awe-inspiring. New industries, partners, vendors, workers, and their families are pouring into the area in unprecedented numbers. The new global village of the South is a challenge to New Southerners, but also to long-time Southerners who want to preserve the unique culture of the region. The global village has made its home in Southern backyards, in our internet connections, and it is the workplace of our future.

The goal of this book is to meet the challenge of the global village of the South. *Going Southern* is organized into three sections that will be released separately as a series and finally, as a compilation book. Each of the three books in the series builds on the information, analyses, and tips of the earlier sections. The strategy for acculturating New Southerners is based on the principles of global leadership development, cultural anthropology, and intercultural training. The iconic Southern storytelling format provides easy access for Southerners and an introduction to a key communication mode for newcomers. Typical of storytelling, the chapters will entertain as they educate and engage as they draw the reader into cultural competence. The practical tips at the conclusion of each story will answer many of the common questions of New Southerners and demonstrate to Southerners the expectations and challenges of the newcomer.

- WHERE & WHEN: How does geography and history shape the region that is now known as the New South?
- WHO & WHAT: What are the demographics in the South? Who is here and what does this mean for you?
- HOW & WHY: How should cross-cultural communication skills, verbal and non-verbal, by applied to the workplace in the South? Why should we understand the hot issues in managing national and international teams with Southern members?

**Who needs this book?**

If you fall into one of these categories, you should be reading Going Southern: 1) Expat and Transplants, 2) Southern

Professionals who work with them, and 3) Returning Southerners.

1) The New Southerner needs a level of comfort in the South that ensures productive use of time and energy invested here. Companies such as Volkswagen Chattanooga arrange for an acculturation program for its international executives. This is not an option for most executives in small- and medium-sized businesses who have ties to the international industry: vendors, employees, and consultants. In addition, students, interns, and faculty coming into the South are often in the same position of fending for themselves. Many underestimate the culture shock they will experience; these expats and transplants will need a no-mess guide.

   Many New Southerners bring their families with them. While they are at work or school, their families need to feel at home quickly and to create normalcy in their lives. *Going Southern* offers insight into the most pressing issues that internationals face in the South. The book's storytelling format is the basic communication style that they will encounter from their first days here.

2) Southern professionals will increasingly deal with our newcomers: Human Resource officers, educators, trainers, salespeople, banks, healthcare providers, nonprofits, recreation providers, and a

host of other organizations that interface with a diverse population. Many Southerners feel that they already know their culture well. For them, the issue isn't knowledge. The challenge is how to be aware, to articulate, to negotiate, and to work successfully with the massive wave of newcomers. Southerners will laugh at the stories in this book, and then construct their own stories in ways that have a global interface. The tips in *Going Southern* will prepare them for being on the front lines of change, for serving as tour guides to the new Southern global village, and for the pursuing cross-cultural training necessary for global leadership.

3) For Returning Southerners, the guide will help reconnect you with a rapidly changing region. This isn't the South you left and you have a major role to play in its future. By leaving and coming back, you have acquired new skills and a more objective perspective on Southern culture and society than natives who never left. You may not know it yet, but with a little training, you can become a valuable asset for shaping the region's future.

## Chapter 2: *The Decision: Going Southern, Y'all*

Are you considering moving to the South and wonder if your journey here will be successful? If you're moving your business here, if you're moving your family here for a job, if you're moving your professional self to the South, you'll need a few words of wisdom, Southern-style. Even if you once lived in the South and are now returning, a refresher course is in order. So here's some down-home advice from someone who came to the South for a job, fell in love, and never left. That would be me. Maybe it's my training as a cultural anthropologist that fuels my fascination with Southern culture. Or maybe it's that after 15 years of living and working in Chattanooga, Tennessee, I feel a deep sense of belonging in the South and gratitude for the opportunities it has given me. I am also eager to bring other newcomers on board.

Embrace the choice! I had three major concerns about relocating here. There is nothing like relocating to bring regional diversity issues to the forefront. My concerns are questions that most professionals and entrepreneurs ask themselves before moving from their country or region. First, do I see my family and me as happy in the geography of the environment? Second, will I like the people and feel that we can work and live together comfortably and productively? Last, but certainly not least, is there a match between the mindset of the region and my vision for future professional and business success?

Here in the South, questions like these are not answered with bullet points. The story is the preferred and dominant mode of Southern communication. Storytelling is an art; festivals are built around it and open mike nights help groom storytellers weekly. It's no coincidence that the headquarters of the National Storytelling in Organizations Association is in Tennessee. So, in good Southern fashion, I will answer these questions with a story or two of my own.

When my husband, Earl, and I decided to come to Chattanooga for an interview, we took the opportunity to drive around the area. I was drawn here by the very thing that will attract you to the South, too. The beauty of the region is phenomenal. You can spend every weekend and every vacation taking in the natural beauty of the South and still want more. Southern mountains, rivers, and towns called me like the Sirens in the *Odyssey*. I fell in love with the sight of barges on the Tennessee River, fisherman in rowboats on the lake in the shadow of Signal Mountain, one of several that ringed the city and the Chickamauga Dam that controlled the flow of water. But nothing caught my imagination like the lush green hills, full of spring colors. There were infinite shades of green and flowering trees of white and pink everywhere. Even the parking lots, hospital sidewalks, and highway exits were full of leaves, blooms, buds, and birds.

Listen to the music! No wonder Southern music is full of odes to the region! It's hard not to hum tunes that echo the Mighty Mississippi and Rocky Top, the City of New Orleans, and Memphis. Yes, Georgia is on my mind when I can virtually walk over the border. Musicians are one of the South's most enduring exports and an advance cheering section. Southern music takes the region's beauty to people and places totally unrelated to the South, but happy to imagine it. Yes, I had heard the music, too. There was no question about its beauty. I could see us happy in this environment. But would the impressive geography be enough for a career here? What about the people?

Anticipate friendliness! Having dinner in people's homes, coffee in the restaurant, even walking on the street is an exercise in smiling. Southerners have a well-earned reputation for being welcoming and hospitable. When they smile, it's not a subtle move. Everyone's face lights up--theirs and mine. From the first phone call arranging the interview, the people we met were gracious and welcoming. They reminded me of my childhood in Bermuda where relationships were an art form forged by spending a lifetime together on twenty-four-ish squares miles. They reminded me of my mother. My 85-year-old Aunt Polly calls her a saint; I call her the original Island Girl, full of sunshine and kindness.

Mom was born gracious and was a strong believer in giving everyone the benefit of a doubt and applying positive reinforcement whenever possible. So, I felt a sense of coming home with the flood of compliments like, "Great resume!" and "I can hardly wait 'til you join our club, group, event; fill in the blank." I knew that no job is without its challenges, but Mom had been very firm about there being a time and place for such things. Thanks to her, I just said "thank you" to the kudos on my education and the enthusiasm about my achievements. And, while I tend to get terribly embarrassed by very personal compliments, I withstood those, too. Perhaps even then, I was more Southern than I realized because I fell for every compliment that came my way. And I completely put aside my natural reserve when one of my interviewers said, "I love your necklace."

Enjoy the compliments! So often, it's the small things like this compliment that push us to chart a course for the South. The jewelry in question was a coral necklace given to me by my grandmother years ago when we still lived in Bermuda. The necklace brings back memories of growing up as a British colonial, celebrating Empire Day, basking on pink beaches, and swimming in the crystal-clear lagoon at Horseshoe Bay. Not that childhood was the always the easy-going life of a semi-mermaid. We were too much in the public eye for that. My family was one of a handful of Jewish families who'd lived and worked on the island for generations. We served as an informal, unofficial Jewish consulate from our home, a lovely old house called Shadow Lawn. Driving by a street in Chattanooga called Shadow Lawn Drive and seeing a town house for rent was both jarring and reassuring.

I was not daunted by the prospect of adjusting to the South. Or at least I told myself that I shouldn't be. I had learned about cultural adjustments as a kid when my parents inserted us into the New York City area. Getting news of the move from our twenty-four-square mile island to one of the largest metropolitan areas in the world felt like being on the Titanic and hearing, "We hit a *what?*" I weathered that move, and the next one to Boston for college, and then to Cincinnati, Chicago, Rockford, and Tulsa. Having mastered being an American in such diverse locations, I knew that my voice would be the first cultural roadblock in relocating here.

Let the accent grow on you! Nothing gave me away as a new arrival more than the way I spoke, even as a kid in New York, fresh off the prop-plane from Bermuda. Americans think they speak English, but anyone brought up British knows better. I was able to finesse the written word with its strange spelling. Americans drop the *u* from words like "colour" and "flavour." But my non-American figures of speech were fair game for playground scuffles. I caused a near riot by using the word "obliged" twice in an oral book report presentation. And, I found out the hard way that while "quite" was an acceptable British response to virtually anything, it's a surefire way to annoy Americans of all ages.

Then there was the New York habit of speaking as if the house were on fire. Everything had to be said a quickly as possible in case we all dropped dead in the next few seconds. There was also an apparent difference in DNA that allows New Yorkers to speak very loudly for as long as they desired and under any circumstances. My attempts to keep up left my poor vocal cords behind in the dust. My voice was an early casualty in going American and I had to accept being speechless for days, literally.

Buy time to acculturate by acknowledging publicly that you know you sound strange, that you're working on it, and could use some help. And advise your children to do the same. When I was a kid, this straightforward approach didn't occur to me. I bought time by learning to swear and curse with the best of the rowdies at school. I don't know what ever came over me. Everyone was so shocked, they forget about the slow, British speech. Please find a strategy other than cursing; it will not go over well in the South.

Over the years and the moves, my speech took on the flavor of the local culture and I dropped the swearing. I considered my acculturation a success when my voice is a comfy match. The cultural anthropologist in me knows that language habits are like cultural artifacts, expressions that capture a culture like a snapshot in time. If your speech mirrors the speed, decibel level, soft vowels, lilt and sentence structure of a culture, then you mirror the culture itself. Nothing says where you're from and where you belong like the way you speak and sound. However, we know that a child can pick up speech patterns far more easily than an adult can. Adults who often end up sounding like a parody of the real thing invite ridicule, or at least a few jokes at their expense. In the South, it's often enough to not shout and not aim for speed.

Breathe! The flavor of a culture seeps into your speech even when you're not too crazy about it. I started to sound like a true Bostonian when I was at Harvard. I was mercifully quick to drop the "Haavard Yaad" accent when my time there was over, but it was alarming to think that I fit in there for a few years. As a brutal boot camp for the mind, Harvard has few peers. And when I left, it never occurred to me to seek work there. Yet, my dad was originally from the Boston area so I suppose that broad "A" is lurking in my blood. Dad had been a translator during World War II and had lost the Boston accent somewhere between the French and the German he used as a military intelligence officer. He was big on languages being spoken with precision and informed me when I started studying French at age 12 that no child of his would speak lousy French and live. He felt the same about a Southern accent.

Dad's language was refined to the point of regal and you might think that mentioning him is totally irrelevant to the down-home style of the South. Dad didn't even speak the down-home language of his fellow Lithuanian immigrants, Yiddish. At least he never actually admitted to it. Yiddish isn't just a Jewish Eastern European's language. It does double duty and symbolizes not just ethnicity, but class. Both grandfathers spoke some Yiddish, but my grandmother knew only a few words. Her family, the Swigs, arrived in America much earlier, became affluent, educated and Americanized. Dad was first American-born generation of poor immigrants, but he was also an educated Harvard man looking to the future, not the past.

So how did I acquire my love of Yiddish? I had a pretty good dose of the language during the recession of 1971. My college grad friends found themselves working at the local gas station and I got a job as a Gal Friday in the Garment District. Back then, the Garment District was still a vibrant Jewish retail tradition In Manhattan and I had a chance to experience my roots big time selling in the *schmatte* (rag) trade. My affection for Yiddish would be the wind in my sails for years to come and I would come back to it in the unlikely environment of the South.

My journey took me to the mid-west before coming to the South. My dad became a systems management consultant at the Cincinnati headquarters of Federated Department Stores. It was in Cincinnati that I took my first job as a nonprofit director and Dad sat me down with a few words of wisdom about doing community work. The words turned out to be all in Yiddish, a colorful stream of curses that rolled easily off his tongue. "*Gae cockin afen yum,*" Dad taught me. "You'll need to tell some people, 'Go sh*t in the ocean.' Also, *Gae gesundt,*" he said. "Go with God. Lord knows you'll need His help working in nonprofits."

The nonprofit road soon led from Cincinnati to Chicago and a Masters degree in Urban Planning & Policy; a MUPP, which sounded much better in a flat, mid-western accent than anything I had in my arsenal. I was getting older and I never quite absorbed the Chicago accent. My classmates decided that the only possible explanation for my awkward speech was that I was actually French, but wouldn't admit to it. My toddler daughter sounded mid-western almost immediately, prompting my exasperated father to ask her, "Why do I say 'Chicago' and you say 'Chicaaaago'?" Her response to this ex-military, intimidating man was, "Because you're a ding-a-ling." It's humbling or comforting, depending on your perspective, to know that your child acculturates faster than you can and with more confidence and flair.

Ah, the expectations! I immediately fell in love the soft speech of the South and was confident that even though middle-aged, I'd blend in with the accent. My grandfather had grown up in the South, although it wasn't the first thing I associated with him. Rather, Gramp and his parents were part of a massive immigration wave of Jews from Eastern Europe in the early 1900s. He acquired the Irish last name "Malloy" at

Ellis Island and an 8th grade education in Virginia. Yet, Myer M. Malloy had a remarkable talent for the Old Soft Shoe like the famous Bo Jangles and could waltz like a true Southern gentleman. His soft voice never ended "ing" with a hard *g* and the word "pillow" was charmingly "pulla." Yes, he was a tough entrepreneur, one of Bermuda's first professional realtors. But he was as good a social animal as any true Southerner; shooting craps with the priests, dancing with the ladies at the nightclubs, and playing his auctioneer skills on behalf of everyone from the American government to the local church.

Surely, Gramp's genes would surface once I was in the South and my soft voice would adjust quickly. It couldn't take long to acquire that beautiful Southern drawl: that charming, musical speech that symbolizes the South so well. I'd throw in a few y'alls, and, pretty soon, no one would be able to tell the difference between me and a native Southerner. It never happened and my odd mix of accents was ascribed to my having lived in Virginia, which was only a daydream of my youth. It never happened.

As any professional or entrepreneur would ask, I finally came to the question of whether my background, education and experience and the local opportunity were a good match. The Jewish Community Federation had rented offices in the small township of East Ridge in Hamilton County, just outside Chattanooga city lines. During World War II, there were 5,000 Jews in the area;

now there were 1,500. Their large community center had been sold; the upkeep was major and the population not growing. Yet, there was a vision of building a new center, attracting new Jewish businesses and professionals. Despite the obvious challenges, there was energy, optimism, and determination.

Was the forward-thinking vision of the Jewish community echoed elsewhere in the Chattanooga area? As we took in the local sights, as good tourists should, Earl and I saw the aging infrastructure that is a frequent sight in the South. The hills and mountains, lakes and rivers have transportation and industrial sites that evoke eras of long ago. Earl was a design engineer who had worked internationally and the infrastructure was his main interest. He marveled at the engineering the trolley that had once taken people from the top of Lookout Mountain down to the city area. Yet, it's now a fun ride, like the kind you might find in an amusement park. Much of the city was older: the warehouses by the river, the shops along the main streets, and the old steel mills. Once a famous railroad hub, no passenger trains came in or out of the city. The trains at the Chattanooga Choo Choo were now museum pieces and hadn't moved for years.

Appreciate the vision! We considered whether our lives would be folded into the quaint, living museum that we saw in the older parts of town. Yet, we also saw a New South emerging as we drove through the streets of Chattanooga. We came to a modern glass structure of the city's aquarium. Built in abstract-style architecture, it was obviously a hub of tourism, fed by an electric shuttle service. It sat next to a state-of-the art IMAX Theater and streets that were paved distinctively and attractively. The air was fresh and clean, far from the reputation the city once had as one of America's center of pollution. Our hosts then took us to the arts district where the museums, cafes, and outdoor sculpture overlooked the Tennessee River. Someone was looking to the future of the city. We learned that while initiated by the city's leaders, the renaissance was a community effort. We saw years' worth of results from the process and had seen similar efforts in other small Southern cities we visited. This is why economic development in the South is so dynamic and why people like me, and you, are willing and eager to risk so much to become part of this region's future.

Yes, I understood that the reality is always different from what you experience on the surface during a visit like ours. That's something that anyone who has relocated or even contemplates such a move will understand. But I was sure that we could navigate this culture, get results, and become part of the great future I saw for the South. The decision was made. Earl and I started packing and prepared for the journey South, for *Going Southern*.

Since making that decision 15 years ago, much has been experienced and much learned. My time here prompted an inner journey from advocate for a culturally diverse group to a professionally advocating cultural diversity and, finally, to an intercultural trainer in a new global village. Given the influx of nationals and internationals into the South, my focus is now on cross-cultural communication and the intercultural skills needed to get results. Here are my stories and some words of wisdom for New Southerners and those contemplating *Going Southern*.

May the surprises that I uncovered and the secret meanings I discovered help make your journey to the South memorable, your time here productive, and your contribution to the South meaningful. And the first piece of wisdom I'm sharing is that never before will the stories of your father and your family be appreciated as they are here in the South. The South is a place where history is alive, memories are inspiration for the future, and family is a living, breathing creature no matter the toll of death and time.

## Chapter 3: *The Intersection: Where Geography & History Connect*

The first challenge in training New Southerners is trying to answer the question, "Exactly what is the South?" The explanation tends to be all over the map, literally. I appreciate the confusion underlying the iconic term "The South." Growing up in Bermuda in the fifties, I had only a vague interest in America and virtually none in the South. I considered myself a British colonial, celebrating Empire Day at the Bermuda High School for Girls. My mother liked to pretend ignorance and referred to the United States as "the Colonies," even though she had attended Radcliffe/Harvard. She was a great admirer of Fred Astaire and Ginger Rogers and the sophisticated New Yorkers in their movies. My image of America was shaped by those movies and the cowboy flicks at the kids' matinee: Hop-along Cassidy, Roy Rogers, and Gene Autry. Nothing about America could compete with that combination of New York City and the Wild, Wild West.

When we moved to the States, my understanding of the South consisted of only a vague sense of the Southeastern seaboard as the path Gramp took getting to Bermuda. My grandmother had an upper-class Bostonian attitude towards the South. It simply didn't exist. My dad's attitude towards the South was more nuanced. His father had sold shoes and he was a traveling salesman for much of his life. Grandpa Will had taken my dad with him on a sales trip into the South, including Chattanooga, during the Depression. The combination of cultural difference and the semi-rural poverty made a lasting impression. When it came time for me to apply to colleges, he refused to sign my application to the College of William and Mary in Virginia. "No child of mine will be caught dead south of the Mason-Dixon Line."

I didn't ask for a definition of the Mason-Dixon Line. Apparently, the South, however you defined it, was no place for the daughter of a Bostonian. We never referred to ourselves as Northerners and certainly not as Yankees. Those were considered Southern terms, holdovers from a Civil War that was so long ago that anyone connected with it had died. Weren't we all now "Americans"?

Yet, even in the modern United States of America, the Mason-Dixon Line decided my fate. For many years, I went along with the pretense that the South didn't actually exist. I understood that the silence was a socially acceptable, Northern euphemism for "Hell, no!" to the plantations, Civil War, slavery, segregation of the South, not to mention the wariness about what lurked behind that drawl. But my fascination with the South grew with the books that I read. How ironic that it was my Yankee, but highly literate, father who provided me with the writings of every Southern author that ever lived. It's not surprising that I fantasized surviving and thriving south of the Mason Dixon Line.

Having understood the meaning of the Mason Dixon Line all my life, I never felt the need to define it precisely until I became an intercultural trainer for international executives coming into the South. Yes, explaining the geography of the South should surely be a basic component of such training. How difficult could that be? And so I opened a few history books and turned to the map section. Thus, I began a journey that is still in the making. Where is the South? The Real South? And how much "Southern" is required to qualify?

It's a popular misconception that the Mason Dixon Line originated during the Civil War era. While it is associated in the American mind with the delineation of North and South with an emphasis on mapping slave-owning states, this was not the original intent. Rather, Charles Mason and Jeremiah Dixon were hired to settle a property dispute associated with the colonial era that extended well after the Revolutionary War, regarding land granted by the King of England in the 1600s. The colonies granted to William Penn (Pennsylvania) and Calvert (Maryland) overlapped and the two families had been in British courts, trying to settle the case for decades. When the decree came down as to the location of the boundaries, Mason and Dixon were imported to map the precise coordinates of the agreement on the map.

Mason and Dixon were an early experiment in bringing in internationals to create an American product. It took them four years and given the various unexpected issues of terrain, weather, and native inhabitants, they never did quite finish. Over the years, The Mason-Dixon Line has been defined differently, but there is general agreement that it runs east-west through the Southern border of Pennsylvania, and north-south between the borders of Maryland and Delaware. Whatever disagreement there is on details, there is no doubt that Mason and Dixon left an indelible footprint. The physical footprint included stone markers at 1-mile and 5-mile intervals, some of which are still visible. The more enduring footprint was a demarcation between the Northeast and the Southern mindset. The most famous marker of the Line may well be the South's new nickname in honor of its surveyor, Dixie's Land.

It's amazing to me how well known "Dixie" is around the world. The internationals coming into the South are rarely interested in the history of the Mason-Dixon Line as per the Revolutionary War era. I understand their boredom. I wasn't interested either, especially coming from Bermuda, which kept British rule. But the word "Dixie" catches our attention. There are few words in this country as emotionally charged, with as much baggage and associated imagery as "Dixie." And there may be no other American songs so well known, but so seldom sung about Dixie Land that begin "Way down yonder in the land of cotton." The virtual anthem of the Confederacy of the South is loved and feared, depending on your perspective, but it's definitely well known. Icon Elvis Presley born in Tupelo, Mississippi and raised in Memphis, Tennessee recorded Dixie. Thanks to YouTube, his emotional rendition of "Look Away, Dixie Land" is posted permanently.

You might think that the Civil War and slavery issues surrounding Dixie would be lost or at least muted after 150 years. It doesn't take more than a short drive around the neighborhood to see why that's not the case. The neighborhood is down the road, across the street, and up the hill from my house. I'm talking about Missionary Ridge, an area of beautiful old houses and awesome panoramas of the valley that is the City of Chattanooga, divided by the meandering Tennessee River and ringed with small mountains that are almost permanently green. Missionary Ridge was also the site of one of the most famous battles of the Civil War.

As Earl and I drive along the narrow two-lane street that winds around the hillside, we stop the car to read the various plaques, signs, and markers that dot people's front yards. Each sign is a short documentary of what happened in this battle. With exquisite detail, we learn from one sign that on Nov. 25, 1863, "General Stewart's division (troops from Georgia, Arkansas, Alabama, and Mississippi) occupied the line of works east of Chattanooga Creek with General Breckenridge's division on its right. The night of Nov. 24th, it was ordered to Missionary Ridge and posted with its left near Rossville Gap. In the afternoon of Nov. 25th, its position was attacked on the left and left rear by Hooke's command, and in front by the divisions of B.W. Johnson and Sheridan. Being thus compelled to yield position the division retreated towards Ringgold." Signs like this one crop up along the road at regular intervals, punctuated by a few statues and what look like grave markers.

Yes, the scenery is eye-catching, but the ancient cannons are even more noteworthy. Some face the road and you look directly into their barrels as you drive by. Others point out over the ridge itself and still others are targeted to someone's front door. It's forbidden to move them. The cannons are protected cultural artifacts, national treasures. They are the property of and the responsibility of the Chattanooga Chickamauga National Military Park. The headquarters, museum, and main sites are located across the border in Georgia, but the history it preserves is ever-present. We feel it come alive as we take a leisurely, early evening drive to check out what's blooming.

On Missionary Ridge, geography continues to be defined by the Civil War, as is the mindset. Keep in mind that many Southerners prefer the term "War Between the States" and occasionally, "The War of Northern Aggression." The loser in any given war is more likely to remember the details and keep them alive than the winner. And the details on the plaques are horrifying to read with the number of men who were injured, who died, and the number of horses that were killed. I can't imagine what it must have been like to do battle on this scale on these gentle hills. And I was speechless when I saw the miniature size of the Chickamauga Battlefield farmhouse that legions of men on both sides fought to the death to capture.

It's not surprising that many people define the South by listing the States that formed the Confederacy during the Civil War and fought against the North. As with most elements of my stories, figuring out which states those were is not as easy as it looks. Yes, there were seven original Confederate states: Alabama, Georgia, Louisiana, South Carolina, Texas, Florida, and Mississippi. Not everyone in every state was in agreement and, contrary to popular belief, not every pro-slavery state seceded from the Union. Factions in Maryland tried to join the confederacy, but they were stopped by federal troops. Maryland fell into the category of "border states" like Delaware, Kentucky, and Missouri. Virginia split into two states with West Virginia going for the North and Virginia remaining with the South. Arkansas and North Carolina joined Virginia in the confederacy. And after much debate and many demonstrations for and against secession, Tennessee also joined them.

The misery of the Civil War is well captured on Missionary Ridge, but so I could see the juxtaposition of old and new, I traveled to one of the epicenters of the early Civil War, Fort Sumter. The battle of Fort Sumter was over quickly, but the hostilities leading to it had been building up for months and the impact lasted for years. As I boarded the ferry in Charlestown, South Carolina for the short ride to Fort Sumter, I was surrounded by tourists of all ages, but particularly families with young children more eager to eat the snacks served on board than to see where history had been made. As the kids fought over the juice boxes and chased each other with candy bars in hand, we made our way up the channel.

We came to the manmade island with the ruins of an old fort as our guide droned on about how the federal government used tons of rock and built this island to defend the US Marine border from 1829-1845. After more droning on about the battle that ended in a Confederate win in 1861, the ferry turned around and proceeded back to the dock.

I've often wondered if the trip back was planned or if it came as a surprise to the captain, but we went further than the dock. We began to make our way towards The Citadel, one of America's early military academies whose students were used to beef up the confederacy's military during the Fort Sumter battle in 1861. A voice came over the loudspeaker that we were to put away all cameras. Anyone caught taking pictures would have their cameras confiscated by federal government officers. Nor would we be allowed to take notes on what we saw; all paper and pens would also be confiscated.

The ferry then navigated its way through an armada of military vessels. We were surrounded and dwarfed by naval battle ships. There was total silence on board as we reached The Citadel and quietly turned around, heading for the dock. The kids were like statues, watching the incredible naval might of the US Navy on display. So were the adults as we took in this lesson that as unintimidating as Fort Sumter may look now, the strategic placement of military might in this channel should not be underestimated. Not then and not now. The Atlantic Southeastern states are both a part of the South and a maritime sub-culture.

The sub-cultures in the South are as distinctive to Southerners as they are confusing to outsiders. The terms are not precise; the interchangeable South and Southeast cause frustration. The colloquial terms of Dixie and Dixie Land that they hear in Southern music is appealing, but without the frame of reference of the Southern understanding. The differentiation between Southeast and Southwest is unclear. Researching them online reveals a multitude of definitions and possible definitions. One of the more confusing designations is "the Deep South."

A British website about the Deep South defines it as Alabama, Georgia, Louisiana, Mississippi, and Tennessee. However, most Americans would not agree with this list. Some would go with the first seven states to make up the Confederacy: South Carolina, Mississippi, Florida, Alabama, Georgia, Louisiana, and

Texas. Others will go with the States that historically produced cotton. Still others, those in Louisiana, will refer to their state on the Gulf and therefore, it should have its own designation as "the Deep, Deep South." Regardless of the specifics, those who feel they live in the Deep South will often refer to it as the "Real South."

In measuring Southern-ness, most Americans acknowledge that Florida and Texas had immigration patterns that separate them from the South. They might include the Florida Panhandle in the Deep South, but Texas is not a good fit. When I asked a local businessman if Texas should be included in the South, the first response was silence. Then came the comment, "Maybe, but I don't think we really want them here anymore than they want to be here."

History and geography make Texas technically part of the South, one of the original Confederate States. But the New Southerner should understand the distinction between the Southwest and the South. The Southwest had more in common with the West after the Civil War; much of it was still wilderness. The lore of the West is so powerful that it can fill up our image of America. Many of my trainees were far more fascinated by the West than the South.

I understood how they felt. I, too, daydreamed about cowboys when we moved to New York City and was incredibly disappointed that there wasn't a ranch in sight. I immediately asked, "When can I see an Indian?"

(This was before "Native American" became the accepted terminology.) Not getting anywhere with that, I made what I thought was a reasonable request was for a pony. My father, after he stopped laughing, pointed out that a 3rd floor walk-up apartment in New York was not a good place for a horse. He only laughed harder when I informed him that I was flexible and would keep the pony at the local stable when I wasn't riding it. I reacted as any seven-year-old would. The tears flowed along with a few sobs and wails, always my dad's undoing. Do not mess with the daydream! I was soon presented with, and comforted by, a huge beach towel with a cowgirl on one side and a Native American girl on the other.

Relocating, no matter the age, is as much a mindset as a matter of geography and nowhere is that more so than in the South. The understanding that the South is "a state of mind" is a well-known fact even internationally and is featured in the British Deep South website. Ask a Southerner if this is true and they will simply nod "yes," as if it's a given and needs no explanation. Regardless of how you define the South, Southeast, or Deep South, you are tapping into a cultural pride that is strong and deep. Showing respect towards the South is vital here. Express disdain, or even indifference, and you court disaster. There won't be tears; however, an informal poll of Southerners about advising newcomers to the South revealed that the number one tip was to show respect. The second most frequent tip was to learn Southern ways. In reality, the two tips are virtually indistinguishable in the Southern mindset. They are shorthand for "learn about us and like, respect, and identify with us."

# Chapter 4: *The Names: Why Native American History Is Relevant Today*

The Native American names across the geography of the South are impossible to miss. States, cities, counties, rivers, and streets are named for or by the tribes that once lived here: Alabama, Biloxi, Cherokee, Chickamauga, Etowah, Muskogee, Natchez, Ooltewah, Seminole, and Sequatchie. You don't have to look far to see evidence of the 29 Southeast Native American tribes listed online. Here in the South, there are streets, libraries, sports teams, newspapers, and schools with Native American names. A key question for New Southerners should be whether there is any relevance of this to their success here.

Non-Southerner Americans coming into the area are a bit mystified by the names and constant reminder of Native American history. Knowledge of the Southeastern tribes is minimal, although there is a general understanding that they were rounded up and marched out West. They frequently don't know that one of the destinations was Oklahoma, not far from Tulsa. They're not clear about the ugly, violent nature of the evacuation, but they do know the term for it: "The Trail of Tears." They have an image of the Southeast as devoid of Native Americans and their influence.

Unless they're history buffs, it can be disorienting for non-Southerners to see Native Americans embedded in the regional geography. There are groups now that retrace the Trail of Tears in order to better understand what happened. Having spent three years working in Tulsa, I appreciate the impact of such a trip. The Native American place names are virtually identical in Oklahoma as in the South. It is more than disorienting to see the Cherokee nation's capital in Oklahoma and then see the remnants of it in Georgia. When the Trail of Tears comes alive like this, the pain is stunning.

Most of the Internationals coming into the South have read about the forced evacuation of Native Americans from the area. For them, the physical evidence of their early presence is a pleasant surprise. After asking for confirmation that the names are indeed Native American, the first question is invariably about the correct pronunciation. They do not carry the burden of pain and shame for the Trail of Tears and their excitement is endearing. The second question is earnest and eager: "When can I see a Native American?"

On the surface, there is little opportunity to see the Native Americans that once filled the Southeast. This is true, even for what the European colonists called the "Five Civilized Tribes": the Cherokee, Chickasaw, Choctaw, Creek, and Seminole. If you search the Internet for them, you will likely find yourself online at the Oklahoma Historical Society. The Society's site provides one of the best descriptions of the "civilized" terminology: "… the adoption of horticulture and other European cultural patterns and institutions, including widespread Christianity, written constitutions, centralized governments, intermarriage with white Americans, market participation, literacy, animal husbandry, and even slaveholding. Elements of 'civilization' within Southeastern Indian society predated removal. The Cherokee, for example, established a written language in 1821, a national supreme court in 1822, and a written constitution in 1827."

I had more interaction with the Cherokee when I worked in the Tulsa, Oklahoma area than I have had here in their original home, and for good reason. The Oklahoma Historical Society documents that the removal began around 1802, with continued acquisition of tribal lands and increased demand for voiding tribal claims to it, particularly in Georgia. President Andrew Jackson negotiated with a minority group of the Cherokee, including a removal agreement. Despite the best efforts of Cherokee Principal Chief, John Ross, who won acknowledgement of the Cherokee nation from the Supreme Court, the Treaty of New Echota was signed in 1835 and the removal west went forward by an act of Congress.

On one of our drives around Georgia, Earl and I stopped at an out-of-the-way gas station. There was a small sign pointing to the Museum of New Echota. We had not realized that New Echota was an actual place; it had been the capital of the Cherokee nation that once inhabited most of what we now call "the South." The small museum is near a golf course that was originally Cherokee land. It seems abandoned with only a solitary park ranger visible as he takes out the garbage.

We got out of the car to read the inscription on the stone monument. It told of Cherokee achievements, businesses, and community life. It also told of 15,000 Cherokees rounded up in the space of three weeks. New Echota became a prison with Chief John Ross trying to make the situation as humane as possible. All that's left of New Echota is this out-of-the-way museum. Chief John Ross is memorialized in the names of streets and of the landing in the Tennessee River where he began their journey West. The Ross log cabin home is preserved next to a quiet duck pond behind the Bi-Lo Grocery Store in the city that carries his name, Rossville. There is no ranger, no displays, and no reason to get out of the car.

Although John Ross' home languishes behind the grocery store, International New Southerners have a fascination with Southeastern Native Americans ebbs and flows. They often ask where they can attend a Native American gathering; a powwow. While there are some Native American-run powwows, there are also gatherings sponsored by municipalities that have corporate sponsors. I attended one such powwow at the First Tennessee Bank's pavilion in Chattanooga. A large, covered market/bazaar, there is also space for performances. The traditional circle dances were done in this area while onlookers appreciated the colorful dress and the hypnotic drumming, and some joined the dance.

As I looked around the powwow, my eye fell on the drummer, a middle-aged woman whose eyes clearly met mine. Her face expressionless, she stood quietly as I approached. When I asked to speak to her, to interview her for an article, she just gave me a slight smile. When I handed her my card, she turned it over and wrote her phone number on it. "Call me 'Grandmother,'" she said, returning the card to me.

About a week later, I called the number that "Grandmother" had written on my card. When I tried to introduce myself and refresh her memory of our conversation, she stopped me. "I know who you are. I've been waiting for your call and I've written a poem for you." The poem was about a huge old oak tree with roots that went deep and branches that reach out over them, giving shade and nurturing the plants below. "That's you. See how you nurture the plants under your limbs. But see that the branches cannot reach everywhere. You must choose which ones to nurture and which ones to let go. I and my friends from other tribes will pray for you to choose wisely."

It is this spirituality, this gift of oneness with the land we are in such danger of losing that is behind an increasing willingness to acknowledge our tribal history in the South. Several years ago, Chattanooga created a memorial of ceramic mosaics marking the Trail of Tears at the John Ross Landing. The artwork was done by Bill Glass Jr., a prominent Native American artist and a member of the Cherokee Nation of Oklahoma. Glass says about his art, "The final product is durable and with the addition of glazes for colors and surface textures, I feel like I'm able to create pieces that are relative to a southeastern style of Indian Art with contemporary methods. I work in this style to reflect my Cherokee heritage." Along with the demanding aspects of working with clay, he continues to research the southeast woodland culture through the pre-historic and historic periods. Ancient southeastern motifs provide an art basis to which the Cherokee people are culturally related. "Through design variations of this art style, I am able to produce new imagery that has a relationship to those of old . . . I work with the clay, but do not totally dominate it, letting its spirit coincide with mine..."

What does the interest in Southeastern Native American-named mean for New Southerners wanting to do business here? There are four ways in which cultural competence in this area can be used. First, your ability to pronounce the Native American names of places signals that you've done your homework and are familiar with the geography. If you're not sure, asking about the correct pronunciation is an excellent way to engage Southerners. They will appreciate your interest in learning about the region.

Second, showing up at Native American festivals and visiting Native American monuments will signal your appreciation of Southern history. History is greatly valued in the South, more so than most regions in the United States. If you show that you value that history, you will also be showing that you value the people of the region. The respect that this demonstrates is no small matter to Southerners.

Third, you should assume that your employees, co-workers, vendors, and customers in the South have some connection to our Native American history. Officially, tribal designations come from the federal government and require substantial paperwork. This means that few people in the South are in the position to declare themselves to be tribal members. Unofficially, many Southerners have Native American relatives in their family tree. I rarely train a group without at least one participant including Native American in their background.

Some with Native American ties are Caucasian; some are African American. Some are eager to claim their roots and to help them; many Native American websites enable genealogical and birth certificate searches. Some will prefer to minimize their Native American heritage. That reluctance is rooted not only in the terror of the Trail of Tears period, but in its aftermath. Native Americans who remained in the region were stereotyped, discriminated against, and the object of derision. Jobs were difficult to find and poverty remains an issue.

Not long ago, I was asked to drive out to the hills of Georgia near the Tennessee border and meet with some tribal elders about writing a grant. When I arrived at the small house, I was taken around back to a sweat lodge. On the slant of the hill was a tent equipped with the ability to heat stones and to be filled with steam for hours, perhaps days. The elders had traveled from their reservation in the Dakotas in the hope of obtaining funds—salaries for tribal leaders to maintain this ancient form of spiritual healing.

It broke my heart to tell them that corporations and foundations rarely funded salaries and, in addition, the sweat lodge would be considered a religious activity, also rarely funded. They were devastated and, pointing to a shadowy figure in the doorway, they asked me, "How can we provide cigarettes for our chief?" This scene should not be; I gave them whatever change I had in my wallet.

The Native American issue is complex. Be aware of the multitude of reactions that are possible and tread lightly. I am grateful to the elder for helping me understand at a gut level the difficult position that Native Americans continue to find themselves in the South. How could they not have a strong instinct for self-protection and survival? Ask yourself: if you had Native American DNA, would you keep it private, too?

The connection of the Native Americans to the land is a connection that still persists in Southerners. The frequent distance from the land and the occasional disdain that you might find in a large metropolitan area is not the norm here. The very thing that likely brought you here—the beauty of the region—is an ongoing part of the Southern mindset. Even though there are obvious challenges here, difficult histories, and current inequities among the people, the land and the geography, have meaning on their own. The fourth and final piece of advice coming from the Native American roots is to find a way to experience a spiritual connection with the land. Don't be afraid to express it when you embrace it. To express a love for the land is to express a sense of belonging in the South.

## Chapter 5: *The Myths: How to Navigate the Old South and Avoid Missteps*

The early history of the South is as much with us as current events. Your knowledge of its history shows respect and discernment. Knowledge that goes beyond popular theories and misconceptions is invaluable for navigating the South. Here are six common misconceptions about the early South that you need to know in order to understand conversations about Southern culture, education, politics, and who's who. Not only will this help you avoid major blunders, but there is an added bonus of putting you on the path of some great Southern experiences.

*Myth #1:* The colonization of America began with the landing of the Mayflower at Plymouth, Massachusetts. Every American schoolchild knows about the Mayflower ship that set out from England in 1620, carrying Protestants who were seeking religious freedom. The "Pilgrims" landed at Plymouth, surviving the harsh New England winter with assistance from local tribes, giving rise to our national holiday of Thanksgiving celebrated with a family-oriented, gorge-yourself feast. Yes, but …

*Reality Check*: The English competed with the French and Spanish for land as early as 1584 and had several failed colonies before Plymouth. More importantly, the first permanent English settlement by England in America was not in the South. The English succeeded in 1607 with about 200 settlers at "James Fort," named for King James and later known as "Jamestown." The colony was established by The Virginia Company, which was also given permission to expand it to include land that would later become the state of Virginia and the Bermuda islands. Southerners who can trace their ancestors back to Jamestown 400 years ago are as proud of their roots as the Mayflower descendants are of theirs.

*Must See*: Jamestown no longer exists and much of the original Fort James is underwater. But the owners of the land donated 22 acres of it in 1893 to what is now Preservation Virginia. The remaining acreage, "Historic Jamestowne," is now part of the National Park Service. According to the Associated Press, the State of Virginia recently added 13 new historical markers to the 2,400 markers created since the 1920s. There are plenty of places to visit.

*Myth #2*: Jamestown would have failed if not for the romance between Captain John Smith and Pocahontas. She was the favored daughter of the Algonquin Chief Powhatan. Pocahontas saved Smith's life and brought food to the settlers when they were starving. We know this because of the Disney movie, *Pocahontas*. What a romance, but …

***Reality Check***: It's true that Pocahontas kept the colony alive with food, but it's unlikely that she and John Smith had a mad romance together. Pocahontas was 11 when the English arrived; Smith was 28 years old. Much of Smith's true heroism is less well known than this faux romance. He secured Jamestown's future with his "rude" letters to English investors, demanding food and carpenters rather than rhetoric, threats, and more minor noblemen. The Virginia Company complied, but the provisions and useful emigrants were shipwrecked on Bermuda and delayed for months. Yet, they did arrive with provisions in the nick of time; almost half of the settlers had died. In addition, the ships brought help in the form of John Rolfe, whose wife and child had died and were buried on Bermuda.

It is John Rolfe and Pocahontas who had the great romance. She converted to Christianity, was renamed Rebecca, and years of peace between the tribe and Jamestown followed. Rolfe developed a variety of the native tobacco that would appeal to British tastes. We rarely tell the story of Rolfe and Pocahontas. It was their influence that both preserved Jamestown and shaped its future economy. Yes, enjoy the romance, but remember the key words to the economy of the South: "land" and "tobacco."

***Must See***: Check out the Disney movie, *Pocahontas*. Half of it is total fantasy, but the other half is educational. Altogether, it's great family entertainment and gives insight into the American mindset as well.

*Myth #3*: The "British" founded Jamestown and ruled during the Colonial period (1607-1775). At first glance, this would appear to be a true statement. However, most Americans don't distinguish between the British and the English. The term British covers the English and the Celts: Irish, Scots, and Welsh. And all four emigrated to America, but only the English ruled colonies. The English often implied upper class or nobility, as it did in the case of Virginia. The distinction may be blurred because of the values developed in America. With our democratic ideals, we tend to differentiate between economic classes, rather than nobility and commoner. Are we not all created equal?

*Reality Check*:   Jamestown had the first legislative assembly in America in 1619. There was a considerable disconnect from the English noblemen like Sir Maurice Berkley who helped fund the Virginia Company. Yet, when mismanagement and wars with native tribes threatened the well-being of Jamestown, the King revoked the charter of the Virginia Company and made Jamestown a royal colony. Berkley's son was given the Royal Governorship of Virginia along with 1,000 acres of land.

Governor Berkley gave an aristocratic tinge to the social structure of the South. During the Civil War, England sided with the South because of the similarity. Berkley also gave the South much of its agricultural foundation. He experimented with growing tobacco and cotton: crops that were the foundation of the plantation system.

*Must See*: Check out Virginia Royal Governor Berkley's Green Spring Plantation, which is now preserved as part of the National Park System. And while you're in Virginia, you may want to take a tour of Williamsburg and the College of William and Mary. It's the second oldest university in America, authorized in 1693 by King William III and Queen Mary II.

*Myth #4*: Cotton-growing plantations with hundreds of slaves were the norm. The imagery of the plantation from the movie *Gone with the Wind* fuels plantation fantasies. In addition, according to the Understanding Slavery Initiative (USI), there were 4 million slaves in America by 1860, with 60% of them in the cotton industry. How could the Hollywood-version of the plantation not be a bona fide Southern invention?

*Reality Check*: The plantation model was first deployed elsewhere in the New World by the Spanish, the Portuguese, the Dutch, and the English. It is true that cotton grew plantations to an extent not seen before. The Cotton States defined the region known as the Deep South: Alabama, Georgia, Louisiana, Mississippi, and South Carolina. The Cotton States came also to be known as the Old South, which some say is the real South and more a state of mind than a locale.

Despite the pervasive image of the plantation, it did not totally define the Southern social structure. According to Digital History's research leading up to 1860, "… only 11,000 Southerners, three-quarters of one percent of the white population, owned more than 50 slaves; a mere 2,358 owned as many as 100 slaves." Digital History further explains that slave owners included "African American, mulatto, or Native American; one-tenth were women; and more than one in ten worked as artisans, businesspeople, or merchants rather than as farmers or planters ..." Ironically, neither General Robert E. Lee nor Jefferson Davis of the Confederacy owned slaves, nor did 90% of the Texas militia. Yet, Northerners Ulysses S. Grant and General William T. Sherman owned slaves, as did a third of the Union army. The reality, however, does not lessen the fascination with plantations.

*Must See*: There are many websites (i.e.: USA Today Travel) that offer information about plantation tours. The site includes plantations from the 18th century such as the Destrehan Plantation outside New Orleans. Also in Louisiana is the Myrtles Plantation. L'Hermitage Plantation, known for its violence towards slaves in an era of such violence, is in central Maryland. It is a separate site from The Hermitage, the Nashville, TN plantation owned by President Andrew Jackson. If you are interested in the earlier Colonial era, Drayton Hall and the Magnolia Plantation in South Carolina are from the late 1600s.

*Myth #5*: Slaves used their spare time to help build plantations, loved their masters, and they would still be on the plantations if it weren't for the Yankees and the War Between the States. This was announced to my tour group at the plantation that is now home to the world-famous Spoleto Festival in Charleston, South Carolina. The guide was referring to the spectacular butterfly-shaped lakes on the plantation grounds when she declared them to be a labor of love. She showed us where slaves hid the plantation's silver during the Civil War. For her, it was proof that the slaves loved their masters, the norm in her opinion.

***Reality Check***: Stereotyping that emerged from our history of slavery is considered "Old South" and not appropriate in modern language. Early stereotypes of slaves as simple-minded, lazy, naïve, primitive, servile but joyous were played out in stories, music, and theater. Yet, history shows us that slaves were denied education and rights to their person and families. The docile stereotype should have been laid to rest along with Crispus Attucks, an escaped slave who, in 1770, was America's first casualty in the Revolution against England. Emancipation for slaves wouldn't come for another 95 years. During this period, the Antebellum Era (1781-1860), activism was severely repressed, but there were several notable slave revolts: the Stono Rebellion (1739) in South Carolina, Nat Turner (1831), and John Brown (1859) in Virginia.

***Must See***: Check out the many online resources concerning slavery, i.e. PBS series on Slavery and the *Making of America*. Visit the slave market museum in Charleston to understand the emotion behind this history.

***Myth #6***: The non-aristocratic whites of the early South were ignorant, vicious, and poor. They were Scotch-Irish hillbillies living in the isolated Appalachian mountains of Alabama, Georgia, and Mississippi, or the Ozarks further west. They were rednecks; poor white farmers whose work on the land turned them red with the sun, especially the back of their necks. They grew corn and made whiskey. They feuded like the Hatfields and McCoys. They were rural hicks; ungrateful and dangerous.

The class division is still alive today. In a July 16, 2012 article in Lehigh Valley's newspaper, *The Morning Call*, the reporter links the trends of the current presidential campaign to Virginia's history. The article calls on this early history to explain the class differences highlighted in the campaign. "During the Colonial era, subsistent frontiersmen from the Piedmont, an area roughly equivalent to the Appalachian Mountains, repeatedly clashed with the wealthier urban merchants and plantation owners of the coastal Tidewater region ...As early as 1675, Nathaniel Bacon organized a frontier militia to seize control of Jamestown and dismiss the aristocratic legislature of Virginia." The article compares the frontiersmen to Marxists, stating that class warfare has always been among us. Is there another side to the legacy of these frontiersmen?

***Reality Check***: The early Southern farmers, hunters, and fishermen were uneducated, but they had a set of skills for living off the land. They did whatever it took to survive as pioneers on small, subsistence farms. These are the militiamen who made the difference during the Revolutionary War. These are the coal miners whose hard lives fueled a nation. These are the mountain men who were fiercely independent and amazingly self-sufficient. These were the Scotts and the Irish who fought the English in the Old Country and weren't averse to fighting them in the New World.

*Must See*: The Great Smoky Mountains National Park straddles the border between North Carolina and Tennessee. Its website describes the park as a worldwide attraction for its diversity of plant and animal life, the beauty of its ancient mountains, and the quality of its remnants of Southern Appalachian mountain culture. This is America's most visited national park.

These three groups—the aristocratic landowners, the poor farmers, and the African slaves—are the major players in the early South. Their work and interaction determined the geography and the social structure for the future. They shaped the social structure of the Old South, beginning at Jamestown. They would shape education, religion, politics, economics, and the mindset of the New South. The Old and the New were defined by the dividing line of the Civil War. You might think that the war marked a new era and, in some ways, it did. In other ways, remnants of the Old South linger and echoes still persist. The South teaches us that history is never completely in the past.

**5 TIPS TO HELP YOU BOTH UNDERSTAND THE OLD SOUTH AND NAVIGATE THE NEW SOUTH:**

1. Pay attention to historical sites and museums. They are not tangential to the present.
2. Do not use terms that were offensive in the early South. Many are still offensive today.
3. Do not underestimate the fierce independence and pride in the South. It was embedded in the culture from day one.
4. Check out Hollywood's version of the Old South, but don't take what you see at face value.
5. Accept that the Old South can easily appear in today's newspaper. Read that newspaper carefully. There's more to the local news than meets the eye.

## Chapter 6: *The Choo Choo Factor: How Terminus Was Terminated & Reborn-ish*

There are few Southern exports as enduring as the song, "Chattanooga Choo Choo," which was made popular in 1941 by the Glenn Miller Band and has remained popular ever since. New Southerners invariably ask to take a ride on the famous railroad and are disappointed to find that the train is now a museum. No passenger trains travel on Chattanooga's train tracks today. The Choo Choo is part of history now, but the present and the historical live side-by-side in the South, like the railroad tracks that once shaped it.

Stand in line with us as we buy our "tickets" for a tour of the Museum of Railroads and Civil War History in Kenesaw, Georgia. Hear about the "War of Railroads," and how some stations changed hands dozens of times between Union and Confederate soldiers. Come see the exhibit from the Disney movie, *The Great Locomotive Chase*. Fess Parker stars in this true story of Union spy James J. Andrews and his daring, but unsuccessful, hijacking of a Confederate train from Atlanta to Chattanooga. In those days, Chattanooga was larger than Atlanta, which was intended to be a railroad "terminus" and the hijacking would have been a major blow to the Confederacy.

Don't be surprised when Southerners have an insider's knowledge of such exploits. A colleague shared her personal story when she heard I'd gone to the museum. "My family's oral history says that James Andrews was my great uncle. When he was caught, the Confederates first imprisoned him in Atlanta and then held him in Swim's prison (formerly a slave prison) in downtown Chattanooga. Andrews escaped and was found naked in a tree on an island in the Tennessee River. At his hanging, the gallows was too close to the ground for his tall frame. His feet hit the ground and the executioners had to dig the ground out from under his feet. Then they successfully hanged him, burying him in Chattanooga's National Cemetery."

Andrews was only one of hundreds of thousands of deaths in the Civil War. Burke Davis' *The Civil War: Strange and Fascinating Facts* shows that 7.5% of Union soldiers died, but the South lost 30% of its soldiers along with an accompanying destruction of city and rural life. Henry Grady, the editor of the *Atlantic Constitution*, aptly described, in 1886, the Reconstruction challenge as Southern soldiers returned home, only to find, "… his house in ruins, his farm devastated, his slaves free, his stock killed, his barns empty, his trade destroyed, his money worthless; his social system, feudal in its magnificence, swept away; his people without law or legal status, his comrades slain, and the burdens of others heavy on his shoulders. Crushed by defeat, his very traditions are gone; without money, credit, employment, material or training; and, besides all this, confronted with the gravest problem that ever met human intelligence — the establishing of a status for the vast body of his liberated slaves." My Southern friends tell me that Grady's "Swept Away" speech was the inspiration for the title of Margaret Mitchell's book, *Gone with the Wind*.

Many non-Southerners wonder why there is so little forgive-and-forget for a war that was a century and a half ago. A key piece of the puzzle lies in the post-war period. Far from healing the wounds of war, Reconstruction deepened them, etched the wounds indelibly into the Southern culture. The period is rightly called "The Second Civil War" in the *American Experience* series on public television (PBS). Many who celebrated the end of the war and the abolition of slavery were disgusted with an occupying military force often bent on revenge and the economic exploitation of carpetbaggers. The Association of Tamils of Sri Lanka instructed its members in a 2010 newsletter, "… Carpetbaggers were seen as insidious northern newcomer outsiders with questionable objectives meddling in local politics, buying up plantations at fire sale prices, taking advantage of poor southerners and pushing their alien northern ways on southern politics." The term "carpetbagger" remains a symbol for the arrival of sleazy opportunism.

Given all of the destruction, dislocation, and exploitation, what made recovery possible? The South had two major assets that contributed to the region we see today: abundant natural resources and a transportation network. Minerals and fuel sources included coal, oil, and natural gas. There was iron ore and bauxite used to make aluminum. The rock formations provided gravel, marble, sandstone, and limestone. The South had the raw materials for building roads, for manufacturing, and energy generation. These were the building blocks for "The New South" that Henry Grady dreamed would be "…a diversified industry that meets the complex needs of this complex age" as he popularized the term.

Grady called for industrialization in a eulogy over the nondescript grave of a poor Southerner. "We have got the biggest marble-cutting establishment on earth within a hundred yards of that grave. We have got a half-dozen woolen mills right around it, and iron mines, and iron furnaces, and iron factories. We are coming to meet you. We are going to take a noble revenge … by invading every inch of your territory with iron, as you invaded ours twenty-nine years ago."

The Southeast still produces a substantial amount of US agricultural crops as well as fish, poultry, and tobacco as well as timber supplies. But just as transportation of Mother Nature's products was a major factor in the South's pre-war economy, so it was a major contributor to its reconstruction and to the New South of today.

Transportation modes have morphed with the times. Barge traffic on the bountiful rivers eventually meant dams and controlled waterways courtesy of the Tennessee Valley Authority and the Army Corps of Engineers. Country roads still exist, but highway construction and tunnels changed the landscape a century ago. Trolley cars are rare and replaced by buses. Older highways are being upgraded and widened throughout the South as international industries and accompanying residences and businesses dot the countryside. New highway construction is ongoing as is the onslaught of cars, trucks, and traffic jams.

Railroads are increasingly replaced by airports and jet travel, but their role in the development of the South deserves special attention. Atlanta's website reports that a southeastern transportation system was underway decades before the Civil War. Continually adding tracks and small lines, the Southern Railway was the longest continuous line of railroad in the world by combining and linking nearly 150 railways, spreading across the South and the Allegheny Mountains.

Rail expansion came to a halt with the start of the Civil War and the South's railroads and the economy that depended on them were devastated. Yet, railroad museums describe how most of the railroads were repaired and reorganized even in the harsh Reconstruction Era. Southern railroads instituted many firsts in the industry. The South Carolina Canal & Railroad Co. was the first to carry passengers, U.S. troops, and mail on regularly scheduled steam-powered trains. It was the first railroad to operate at night. The company's tag line became "The Railway System that Gives a Green Light to Innovations." The Southern Railway was the first major railroad in the United States to convert totally to diesel-powered locomotives. From dieselization, to computers, to the development of special cars, the Southern Railway was on the cutting edge of change.

As the railroad system was reborn and re-envisioned, so was the City of Atlanta. In 1877, Atlanta became Georgia's state capital, choosing a fitting symbol as its mascot, the phoenix. Atlanta rose from the ashes of war, reinvented itself not as a railroad "Terminus," but as a hub of highways and air travel. Atlanta completed its small airport in 1929. The sprawling Hartsfield International Airport of today has more traffic than any airport on the planet.

Atlanta is not alone in its resurgence as a transportation hub. Southern seaports were a major resource for centuries, but they should not be relegated to history. New Orleans was a major shipping port since its founding in 1718 and the $2^{nd}$ largest port in America by 1840. New Orleans' trade in slaves and cotton made it a prime target of the Union army, but the port survived the war, just as it survived Hurricane Katrina in 2005. The U.S. Department of Transportation's (DOT) ranked New Orleans as the nation's eighth busiest waterborne freight gateway for international trade by value of shipments in 2008. New Orleans handles nearly $50 billion dollars of international freight. Other major ports in the south, in South Carolina, Charleston, and Georgetown add another $45 billion in business annually.

Despite the booming business provided by the South's transportation infrastructure, that infrastructure is truly a patchwork, a work in progress. I'm driving today from Chattanooga to Memphis, only 268 miles "as the crow flies." New Southerners might assume they could make the drive in about 4 hours. But there is no one road, no crow flying, from Chattanooga to Memphis. Knowing that I have to drive up to Nashville and then down to Memphis, I plan at least an extra hour for the trip. But it's raining and the slick mountain roads mean slower driving so I plan on more time to get there. Fortunately, it's not icy. The South doesn't handle the infrequent snow and ice very well. And while there would be little traffic, especially after residents stock up on enough food to feed a family for a month, some roads are dangerous and it's better to stay home. There is no train. There are small planes, a common Southern resolution of modern transportation problems, but they are expensive, easily delayed by ice, snow, and storms of any kind. Such small distances; such large obstacles!

When we drove through the mountains, we'd stop at the small towns along the way for a snack, gasoline, and a bathroom break. Even though these towns are overtaken by their larger neighbors, and/or become major highway stops, the roads beyond the hotels and fast food restaurants are semi-rural. New Southerners may assume the backwardness is a matter of funding or of logistics. But the isolation is no accident. The local identity is precious and residents fight to maintain their autonomy regardless of the economic cost of the isolation.

My home, the city of East Ridge, Tennessee, was once farmland. Dairy farms and orchards were the norm, but gradually disappeared as its main street grew and a modest mall was built. When the Army Corps of Engineers built a tunnel connecting East Ridge to Chattanooga, the easy access to transportation downtown further urbanized the city. The city has changed from a traditional white rural population to a multicultural mix. It now has one of the most culturally diverse high schools in the county with numerous languages spoken by its students.

East Ridge's rural roots are noticeable in the small, old homes with vegetable gardens, carports, and tanks of propane gas for fuel. Despite its highway accessibility, East Ridge has only one main road beyond which are GPS-defying warrens of narrow streets with no sidewalks. East Ridge citizens proudly preserve their identity. Even as services such as education become county-oriented, East Ridge has its own city council, mayor, a professional city manager, independent library, police and firefighting departments, and its own zip code.

Combinations of Old and New typified by East Ridge are scattered throughout the region and the patchwork of transportation reflects the Southern version of industrialization that Henry Grady envisioned long ago for the region's revitalization. The New South is alive with highways, airports, malls, and industrial parks. However, in the older enclaves, there are mixed emotions about the increased urbanization and traffic. There is worry that the region's natural resources and beauty will be bulldozed, paved, and built up beyond recognition. There is mourning for the loss of Mom & Pop stores as chain stores nudge them out of business. There is resentment when newcomers don't respect traditions and the "we've always done it that way" mindset. There is concern that the global economy means that the jobs of new industries will go to the influx of workers, not locals. There is fear that the South will lose its identity; its culture will fade in memory and value. These are the undercurrents swirling around our Newcomers.

The fear and worry is offset by what this new phase of growth may bring: jobs, technology, training, skills, and economic development. The rebirth of the railroad system that circles Volkswagen's Chattanooga plant symbolizes the hopes for blending the past and the present into a new, promising future. The VW plant is built on a World War II military installation that once funneled troops and munitions from the South to the rest of the United Sates, but was virtually abandoned for years. Now, it is a state-of-the-art manufacturing plant featuring German engineering with American infrastructure, including the newly refurbished train system for delivering cars through the United States.

New Southerners will undoubtedly experience these emotions in a diffuse and usually polite manner. Southerners are hospitable and friendly, but only up to a point. Many newcomers feel the barriers and become frustrated.

**7 TIPS FOR EARNING TRUST AND, POSSIBLY, FRIENDS:**

1. Relax. You are never going to be a "real Southerner." Trying too hard to be one is likely to earn you a reputation for being ridiculous. Authentic interest is appreciated. Fake enthusiasm and phony Southern accents are not.

2. Become a history buff. Your knowledge of history, ability to understand common historical references, and appreciation of the issues are vital elements of cultural competency, and essential for following social trends.

3. Tour the South. Visit the major seaports. See the cultural attractions and festivals. Walk through the museums in small cities and towns. Travel on the major highways and then try some back roads. Take a ride on the passenger railroads preserved in museums. Take a tour of the waterways on an old riverboat. Drive the Natchez Trace Trail, an old Native American trade route from the salt licks in the Nashville area to Natchez, Mississippi in the Gulf Region. Admire what you see and share your admiration.

4. Experience Mother Nature Southern-style. Choose an older home, plant a garden, and buy a dog. Enjoy hiking, biking, boating, fishing, and other opportunities to experience the beauty of the South. Use the weather to initiate

conversation. Learn how to protect yourself and your family in case of heat, storms, floods, and tornadoes and you'll have the added bonus of weathering the Southern climate.

5. Use your GPS. You'll want help finding your way around the South. The cities and towns are not laid in neat grids. The roads and highways reflect the many layers of history in the region. Verbal directions from Southerners are apt to contain references to landmarks they've always known, but which may no longer exist. Caution: Keep your cell phone handy in case your GPS is rendered clueless.

6. Do not try to fit in by adopting traditional Southern symbols or terms. There is too much baggage attached to them for a New Southerner to navigate successfully. For example, do not display a Confederate flag even if the state capital and your neighbor's home or truck sports one. Do not call someone a "carpetbagger." As a newcomer, you have not earned the right to use this Reconstruction Era terminology.

7. When in doubt, ask about time and place. Southerners will be happy to explain the people and events that are mysterious to outsiders, but well understood by long-time residents. For example, during recent droughts, an incomprehensible fight broke out between

Georgia and Tennessee over rightful ownership of a shared river. Gleefully, friends recounted an 1818 conflict over what should constitute the border between the two states and where water from the Tennessee River should go. Two centuries later, the controversy is still alive. Admire—don't criticize—how Southern history, geography, and current events continue to intersect.

# PART II: WHO & WHAT

When you come into the South to live and work, you become part of the ever-emerging New South. In Part I of Going Southern, we looked at geography and history in order to provide definition, background, and structure to your understanding of the South. In Part II of Going Southern, we will look at the people of the South. The success of your efforts to acculturate is directly related to your understanding of the demographics of the South. In this WHO & WHAT section of Going Southern, you will learn about Southern cultural communities, how they evolved, and what the process means for the New Southerner.

## Chapter 7: *The Race Issue: What Outsiders Should Know*

When newcomers, particularly Internationals, ask about race in the South, they do it in a whisper. They know the South's history of slavery here, they know about the Civil Rights Movement and the Rev. Dr. Martin Luther King, Jr., and about Oprah and Usher. What they don't have is a context for understanding the ongoing challenges of race relations. As one trainee asked, "None of you were here originally except the Native Americans, so why does racism persist?"

What accounts for this lack of context? And how can one explain the challenges, misconceptions, and struggles that shape race relations to trainees who are with you for only a few days, sometimes for only a few hours? Much of what is known is from an academic reading of history or exposure to the popular culture of Hollywood. Some of their contacts will tell them that race is no longer an issue. Racial tensions exist for Baby Boomers; the younger generations have moved on. The Civil Rights Movement was appropriate in the 1960s, but it's all about making money now.

Yes, I am one of those Baby Boomers. I joined the Civil Rights Movement in the mid-1960s, picketing in front of the local branch of Chemical Bank, which was then heavily invested in South Africa under the apartheid system. I've tutored in inner city Black schools and danced with an African American dance troupe. I volunteered with SNCC (more about that later) and been a featured speaker at celebrations commemorating The Rev. Dr. Martin Luther King, Jr. Through the years, I've learned many valuable lessons, but one stands out: Outsiders should assume nothing! Much of what the African American community has dealt with will surprise outsiders.

Why deal with any of this history? The reason for doing so is that, even with the best of intentions, your ignorance can lead you into cultural quicksand. The terms you use, the people you hire, the markets you reach, the vendors you contract with, and the people you promote are all part of the ongoing conversation when it comes to the history of race relations. There is one strategy in particular for avoiding assumptions that can adversely impact your business and you personally. It's imperative that you hear from voices within the African American community. Highlighting those voices was a key goal of the American Diversity Report when it was launched in 2007.

One voice from the African American community that appears in the American Diversity Report is civil rights icon, Diane Nash. In a presentation in Chattanooga, she said that the true teachers about African American history and culture are from members of the community. Nash did not want to see their voices get lost in other agendas. "The legacy of the civil rights movement belongs in the hands of the descendants of slaves. Descendants of white slavers, particularly in the South, are taking over the economics of this legacy. People who are activists are not necessarily historians, but they need to join forces." She added, "Blacks need to stay strong within multiculturalism. We need to resist the efforts of the 'think tanks' to water us down with terms like 'people of color.' It may be time to bring 'Black' back."

*Myth #1*: At the end of the Civil War, African Americans entered the political system, equal to other US citizens.

*Reality #1a*: Voting Rights were curtailed for the next century and not until the 1960s did the U.S. Congress pass the 24th Amendment to the Constitution, which states: "The right of citizens of the United States to vote in any primary or other election for President or Vice President, for electors for President or Vice President, or for Senator or Representative in Congress, shall not be denied or abridged by the United States or any State by reason of failure to pay any poll tax or other tax."

*Reality #1b*: There have been only six Black senators to the US Congress since Reconstruction. Some websites list only four because, according to the online African American Registry, the first Black Senator in 1870 did not serve a full term. Further, some do not consider Barack Obama a Black senator because he is part Caucasian.

***Myth #2:*** Race is a Black and White issue.

***Reality #2:*** There were policies in place that maintained race as a Black and White issue. The state bans on interracial marriage were not ruled unconstitutional until 1967 by the U.S. Supreme Court. Not until 2000 did Alabama officially legalize interracial marriage by removing the ban from its state constitution. (About.com, part of the *New York Times* Company). However, a DNA study by Penn State University found that African Americans were, on average, 18% white. This figure does not mean that substantial number of individuals defied the ban. Rather, it represents how African slave women were used by the white masters (blackdemographics.com).

The majority of Americans accept Obama as the first Black President. Historically, individuals with even a small amount of African American DNA were considered Black. The rejection of the racial category for President Obama represents a trend to recognize mixed race as a valid category on its own.

***Myth #3:*** There was no Civil Rights legislation until the 1960s.

***Reality #3:*** Civil rights legislation began during the Reconstruction Period. As reported in the PBS series, courts were reorganized and public school was launched. States were required to give Blacks the vote. But the former slaves were given no land or means for economic stability. The legislation became meaningless and backlash to the intended civil rights was violent.

"Between 1868 and 1871, terrorist organizations, especially the Ku Klux Klan, murdered Blacks and Whites who tried to exercise their right to vote or receive an education …. By the early 1870s, most Southern states had been 'redeemed' -- as many white Southerners called it -- from Republican rule." -- Richard Wormser (PBS.org/*The Rise and Fall of Jim Crow*). The KKK represented rebellion against military occupation and radical social engineering by the North. It was also a violent, vigilante group. Not all roadblocks to civil rights were as violent as the Klan. Some strategies, such as the Jim Crow Laws, were legal, mainstream, and brutal in their effectiveness.

***Myth #4:*** Jim Crow Laws mandating racial segregation mostly concerned separate drinking fountains and restaurants and separate seating on public buses. Jim Crow owes its name to a 19th century minstrel song called "Jump Jim Crow," popularized by a minstrel performer named Thomas "Daddy" Rice who appeared in blackface (About.com). The practices ended long ago.

***Reality #4:*** In 1896, the U.S. Supreme Court declared its support of Louisiana's "separate but equal" segregation law in the *Plessy v. Ferguson* case. This shaped education, running for office, and having a business. Even churches were separate. In 1954, school segregation declared unconstitutional with a Supreme Court case, *Brown vs. Board of Education*. Not until the era of the Civil Rights Act of 1964 did the Jim Crow Laws end. Keep in mind that older individuals experienced the Jim Crow Laws personally. This is not abstract history to them.

***Myth #5:*** Most African Americans left the South long ago.

***Reality #5a:*** Yes, there was more than one wave of migration by African Americans out of the South. The first wave came after the Civil War when plantations were no longer economically viable. About 1.5 million rural, former slaves left the South, using the railroads to migrate to the West and North. A second major wave of migration of five million occurred roughly simultaneously with World War II and in the decades that followed. As per www.blackdemographics.com, almost half of the country's African Americans lived outside the South by 1970.

***Reality #5b:*** Despite migration, the South holds 55% of the country's African American population. Further, outward migration is no longer the trend, according to the site www.blackdemographics.com. As economic development creates jobs in rapidly growing metropolitan areas in the South, African Americans are returning or relocating to the region. Southern cities that are hubs of international commerce include a substantial percentage of African Americans.

Percentage of African Americans Compared to Population per Southern State

| Atlanta, GA | 32% |
|---|---|
| Charleston, SC | 28% |
| Columbus, GA-AL | 40% |
| Jackson, MS | 48% |
| Macon, GA | 43% |
| Memphis, TN | 46% |
| Mobile, AL | 35% |
| Montgomery, AL | 43% |
| New Orleans, LA | 34% |
| Norfolk, VA | 31% |
| Savannah, GA | 34% |
| Shreveport, LA | 39% |

*Source: www.BlackDemographics.com*

***Myth #6:*** African American civil rights organizations operated for a short, intense period during the 1960s.

***Reality #6:*** The passion for organizing for civil rights has been visible and ongoing since Reconstruction. Atlanta was an early center for the Civil Rights Movement. In 1900, Atlanta professor W. E. B. du Bois founded the National Association for the Advancement of Colored People (NAACP). Today, the NAACP is still a major advocacy organization nationwide. The National Urban League was founded in 1910 to assist African Americans from the South in moving to Northern cities and economies. The Urban League continues its advocacy and community assistance today throughout the country.

During World War II, civil rights efforts intensified, particularly among the young, as the nation fought for freedom. CORE (Congress of Racial Equality) was founded in 1942 on a Chicago campus. CORE was active in the South during the sixties in the Freedom Voters Registration project. The murder of three of its civil rights workers is the topic of the movie *Mississippi Burning*. CORE partnered with the SCLC (Southern Christian Leadership Conference) in hosting the student activist group, SNCC, (Student Nonviolent Coordination Committee).

While SNCC is no longer in existence, its passion was unmistakable. Student members risked their safety, sometimes going to jail, for the cause of civil rights. According to Diane Nash, who was one of the founders of SNCC, the students mobilized so powerfully because 1) They were given hope 2) They had a vision 3) They had specific tasks assigned and training to do them. The dream of equality, particularly economic equality, was and continues to be a central organizing theme.

History illustrates the passion for equity again and again. Consider the founding of the SCLC in 1955. A bus boycott organized in Montgomery, Alabama was the catalyst for regional action. Joined by church leaders and black ministers, the Southern Christian Leadership Conference was born and headquartered in Atlanta. The chosen spokesperson was the Rev. Dr. Martin Luther King, Jr., whose leadership helped bring about the historical Civil Rights Act of 1964. Attaining this milestone changed the status of all African Americans, although the quest for equity continues. Martin Luther King Day is commemorated around the country in his honor, but nowhere is it as sacred as here in the South.

For some, the dream of equality took on a fierce self-determination focus. Rather than integrate into the mainstream power structure, there was a desire for Black institutions to rise in prominence, for Black artists to gain recognition, for political clout and recognition. The Black Pride movement promoted self-esteem, prevented abuse, and built community resources without reliance on outsiders. The confrontational element of the movement made some of its leaders highly controversial, including those in the Black Panther Movement, giving rise to counter claims of racism by White critics.

For those interested in in-depth analysis of the history of civil rights, there are numerous resources online. A good resource that lists Black organizations serving the community today and their history is *The Network Journal: Black Professionals and Small Business News* (http://www.tnj.com/lists-resources/black-organizations-and-organizations-serving-black-communities).

## 3 TIPS FOR NAVIGATING ISSUES OF RACE AND RACE RELATIONS:

1. Words matter and carry heavy baggage. Be aware of the language and terms you use when referring to or in working with the African American community:
   - Despite appearing in the organization's brand, NAACP, the word "colored" is never used.
   - The word "Black" as an adjective can be acceptable in the South as in the organization "100 Black Men." While some non-Southern Americans consider it obsolete and prefer other terms, they should not correct its use.
   - Broad terms such as "multicultural" and "people of color" are acceptable in some cases. However, they do not address the African Americans specifically.
   - Self-descriptive terms employed by African American comedians for emphasis and shock value are not for general use. Do not assume because they're said on stage and the audience laughs that you can use them too.
2. Do not assume that regional pronunciation, accents and/or grammar usage indicates a lack of

intelligence. This is true for all Southerners, not only for the African American community. Here is how African American Ph.D. candidate John Stigall explained the dialect issue for the *American Diversity Report*.

British dialects differ greatly from SAE, yet they are almost universally regarded as sophisticated, and for this reason, we gently correct a British exchange student for using an alternative spelling of "favorite." Australian dialects are considered charming at worst, but never as ignorant. However, for some reason when a Black student says "naw bruh" □ (when she or he may be displaying an exemplary knowledge of the subject matter in question) educators often feel the need to remind the student that they are in a school, not in the hood, and about how lazy it is to speak in such an ignorant manner. I believe these sorts of practices should come to an end because there is no good reason to hold one language above another, but this position requires some justification.

One fact to take note of is that certain phrases in African American Vernacular English (AAVE) are more efficiently constructed than their SAE counterparts. For example, consider what linguists call the "habitual *be*" of AAVE. The sentence:

AAVE: He *been* doing his work. With special intonation used for the word *been* is roughly equivalent in meaning to: SAE: He has been doing his work for quite some time.

Thus, we find in this case that SAE is sloppier and more cumbersome than AAVE, and I have no desire to attempt to translate this phrase into the supposedly more sophisticated British dialects.

AAVE includes a large family of sub dialects. Black language differs, depending on geographical region, gender, sexual orientation, age, and class. So having such low regard for AAVE reduces a complex family of Black dialects to mere "thug talk," "street talk," or "slang," which is, in itself, quite lazy and ignorant.

The final and most obvious point is that this brutish scolding of young Black speakers is potentially harmful to their self image. Given that no Americans use SAE at all times, there is no reason why AAVE dialects should be singled out as being inferior in some especially vile way. This does not imply that we should encourage students who use non-standard English to ignore or disregard SAE, but we should encourage what is often called "code-switching," e.g. using SAE in professional and academic social settings and whatever dialect is most effective in more natural social circumstances.

Most people accomplish code switching without formal training, and for this reason, I think a good means of fine-tuning this skill in addition to traditional methods is by using activities that simulate professional and academic social situations such as speeches, job interviews, debates, dinners, and class discussions. All the while, educators should make clear that these sorts of situations are the only time when this dreadful Standard dialect is necessary (I fear that some poor souls have come to believe that they should labor to speak to their friends in SAE). My personal belief is that steps in this direction are more practical and will yield more fruitful results than the current test-oriented approach. More importantly, it represents an attitude of tolerance and understanding that is ultimately better for all of our American students.

3. Anticipate and respect the pride you encounter whether an individual's self-image is multiracial or Black.

Here is a poetic example of multiracial pride written by poet Wendell A. Brown, whose pen name is "The Brown One."

### Nature's Sweet Biracial Child

I am the ginger brown of the Egyptian
The blackness of the Sudan
I am the beauty to which the birds sing
I have the supremeness of the royal Lion

I am the Orchid that adorns the shore of the Nile
And the brightness of shimmering stars
I am the nomad that dwells in the Sahara
I am known throughout the lands afar

I am akin to the American Indians
The Africans and Europeans the same
And yet here I am lost inside of my country
Where no one recognizes my name

My skin is so pure a pecan brown
Blessed with beauty by God aplenty
And yet some try to call me only black
Never recognizing I am akin to many

For I am also the golden brown of the desert
And full of the sweetness of the Nile
The beauty of the worlds continents live in me
For I was born Nature's sweet biracial child

Here are excerpts from a poem on Black pride written by a university student, Darius Myrick. The poem appears in full at www.americandiversityreport.com

### **Proud**

This is me,
My face, my skin, my hair
What I wear, how I think
My interpretation, my life, my story
I'm proud of it.


This is how I think,
With ambition as my ammunition
Intellect as my best friend
Confidence as my right hand man
Swag as my just on the side
And this pencil and paper as my main love
And I'm proud of it

This makes me different
My love instead of hate
My destiny, taking control of my fate
Never afraid to take a chance
Make my own name
A Leader not a follower
Making changes instead of changing myself
And I'm proud of that

I wear clothes that define me not make me

*Deborah Levine*

I have friends that care for a lifetime not a moment
I'm here to earn not to take
I want to achieve not to deceive
My character is my in crowd
My popularity is my own self esteem
I chase goals not material things
God is my best friend
My mind is my soul mate
My life is my reality
AND IM PROUD OF THAT!!!

# Chapter 8: *The Traditionalists: Who Are the Real Southerners?*

Many people coming to America expect to experience the cult of youth and point to the faces on television advertisements as proof it exists. Internationals and Americans alike are surprised that *Going Southern* provides a somewhat different American experience. Age in the South is a matter of both respect and tradition: 1) History is alive and well here, and those who make history are honored. 2) Maturity means allowing for eccentricities. 3) The Southern family teaches traditional manners, which might be considered old-fashioned elsewhere, including "respect for one's elders."

The definition of "old" is flexible in the South. As the famous Mark Twain said, "Age is an issue of mind over matter. If you don't mind, it doesn't matter." One of the fascinating phenomena of the South is that being old can be advantageous. Claiming to be elderly is a common and good excuse for just about anything. When a fifty-something making a presentation at a senior citizens' group was asked why he was there, he responded, "I'm old." Later, when I taught a cross-cultural workshop to a group of five generations, one of the teenage high schoolers said, "It was kinda interesting talking to the old people." The 83-year old in the group responded, "Who you calling old?" Being old in the South means you can say things that would have gotten you into trouble in your younger years.

Who would have thought that hanging out at the physical therapy center would be entertaining? "What happened to your foot?" I asked a fellow patient. "I have a bad case of O.L.D.," replied the man, who was probably a decade younger than I am. One senior citizen proceeded to enlighten us all about the incidence of AIDS in assisted living homes in graphic detail. The young intern is still blushing. Delighting in being outrageous, another senior gave advice for silencing a barking dog in the middle of the night. "Feed it your Ex-Lax (laxative); that dog won't be barking for long." A second young intern, a devoted animal lover, took him seriously and ran after people begging them not to take his advice. The senior was unrepentant in his "Gotcha!" moment.

There is no better place to be if you're older and female than in the South. There is even a special Southern title for older ladies. If you've seen the movie *Driving Miss Daisy*, you'll have heard the title applied. I was a bit startled the first time it was applied to me and was called "Miz Deborah." Surely, I wasn't old enough to have earned the title. But as I realized what perks went along with being Miz Deborah, I settled in. There are offers to carry my groceries to the car, whether I want help or not. Doors are opened, chairs arranged, room temperature adjusted, and the flowery compliments about how lovely I look are frequent. Like any good

Southerner, I don't concern myself with whether the compliments are true.

I am also called "ma'am," as in "Yes, ma'am." My colleagues in other parts of the country are horrified by the mere thought of being called "ma'am." "It makes you sound so old," my counterparts say. They want to be called something more informal, breezy, and youthful. I did try to correct people in the beginning, but soon gave up. I found that it's futile to try and break people of the habit. Further, I unconsciously absorbed the culture that the habit represented. A few years ago, I found myself imperiously insisting that a young man at a local car rental office cease and desist from calling me "Debbie." "That's 'ma'am' to you," I said, and he immediately reverted to his Southern manners.

The Southern attitude toward seniors is not a function of numbers. Most Southern states have a senior population in line with the norm of the country: 13.3%. The attitude is a matter of tradition, generations of tradition. A True, Real Southerner is one whose family extends several generations into Southern history. The Real Southerner frequently has a background that is either rural or small town or both. New Southerners in the workplace are often exasperated by being called "sir" or "ma'am." The habit is deeply ingrained over generations and they find, as I did, that changing the habit for a Real Southerner is virtually impossible.

The transformation from rural traditions to metropolitan sophistication is relatively new in the South. There are few sprawling metropolitan cities like Atlanta. Rather, the South is a place of medium-sized cities and small cities/towns. For example, there are 345 incorporated municipalities in Tennessee, but only 4 major cities. Georgia has 535 cities including Atlanta, with a half million people. Yet, there are only a dozen cities that are even half the size of Atlanta (Georgia Municipal Association). Compare these states with New York, which has 932 towns and claims 71 cities. What accounts for the difference? Historically, the South has large expanses of agricultural areas and mountains. Major corporations would hire workers in the rural areas, but not as managers or in the executive suite. That pattern has begun to change, but a global mindset in the South is resisted by some, and is a target, rather than reality, for many.

In many of the South's small cities, the rural roots are just below the surface. The agricultural mindset and values remain. Hard-working, God-fearing, self-reliant, and neighborly habits are deeply ingrained. Many of the inhabitants have never seen and cannot imagine the anonymity, worldliness, and fast-paced style of a large northern city. A favorite metaphor is to describe speed beyond what is humanly possible as "a New York minute." Use of this saying doesn't imply envy for Big City life, or longing to move that fast, or admiration for those who do.

My new hometown in Tennessee is a great example of a small Southern city-town. You might think I'm referring to Chattanooga, where I do much of my training. And as the smallest of the four major cities in the state, Chattanooga has become a great example of the blend of rural, city, and international hub that is emerging in the South. Yet, for describing a rural roots example, few places are as typical, historical, and iconic as my home in East Ridge, Tennessee.

Not long ago, East Ridge was the site of orchards, dairy farms, and agriculture. Located in Hamilton County side-by-side with Chattanooga, East Ridge is on the far side of Missionary Ridge. The site of a famous Civil War battle and still home to plaques, statues, and cannon memorials, Missionary Ridge once defined Chattanooga's outer boundary. When the Army Corps of engineers cut tunnels through Missionary Ridge generations ago, East Ridge became accessible and almost indistinguishable. Yet, like many Southern suburbs, it defies the label "suburb" with its passion for preserving its rural values and its autonomy.

Most East Ridge houses are small and the roads narrow. The neighborhoods created by the maze of streets are home to as many dogs as people. Yet, the tiny yards are kept with great pride. Planting spring flowers is almost a ritual. Green thumbs abound! And when the growing season is over, many of the modest homes sport ornate decorations during the Christmas season. Homeowners compete to see if their displays will appear in the local newspaper's Christmas list of streets to visit. You'll want to drive around in the dark through the older neighborhoods in the South to see the Christmas decorations, whether you're Christian or not.

Like many small Southern cities, urban planning happens by personality and opportunity. Ringgold Road is the only major avenue in East Ridge. Yet, the City has its own mayor, an elected city council, a library complete with computer/internet capacity, a community center, a paid professional director, a local magazine, police and fire departments. Pockets of wealth aren't far from the pockets of subsidized housing. The seemingly whimsical placement of homes, businesses, and services can defy the non-East Ridger even with a GPS handy.

Recently, East Ridge created an on again-off again history center, a testimony to the South's passion for preserving its culture as well as difficult budget decisions in these challenging times. At the Center, I recorded interviews of prominent older East Ridgers. Talking to the city elders about the past is like being in an old movie. The goats, cows, chickens, and horse-drawn buggies give way to pick-up trucks and multiple cars brimming out of carports. The one-room schoolhouse gives way to public elementary, middle, and high schools. The few shops grow into a mini-shopping mall established by the Osborne family who were successful early in East Ridge's history.

Today, East Ridge has two business councils: a branch of the Chattanooga area Chamber of Commerce and the local ERMA (East Ridge Merchant's Association). Local restaurants host a myriad of civic group meetings. There's always someone or some group meeting about something at Wally's right off the highway exit. For the religious, there are two-dozen churches listed on the city's official web site. Yes, there's something for everyone. Local highlights range from Linda's farmers' market and secondhand consignment stores to the high-tech Rave I-max Theater. This vast social infrastructure serves a city that covers only 8.3 miles, including a 275-acre recreational facility, and has only 21,000 residents.

Families, generations of them, are central to understanding Southern small towns and cities. At one point, East Ridge turned a city-owned building into a History Center to showcase the town's history and those who shaped it. An Oral History Project was funded by the Foundation of the Osborne family and I was hired to interview City elders in order to preserve the East Ridge identity for future generations. The men and women were primarily Christian, mostly white, largely working and middle class with strong rural roots; many still had large vegetable gardens in their backyards. Some were military veterans, others were hard-working professionals, and all were generous in their community work. One interview was with The Reverend Billie Dean, a real sweetheart who truly walked-the-walk and had adopted a young orphaned boy. He was obviously a good role model because that boy, Vince Dean, went on to become a County Commissioner and a TN state legislator.

Cultural diversity is a new development in East Ridge as it is in many Southern towns. The older families are being replaced by younger folks not from around here. The African American population is growing in the City, which many outsiders have yet to comprehend, given the historically mostly White population. There are a growing number of stores and restaurants owned by immigrants: Mexican, Indian, Korean, and Middle Eastern. The East Ridge Library now offers books and CDs in a multitude of languages. East Ridge High School, which specializes in construction and manufacturing skills, is now a county hub for multicultural students and multiple languages.

The influx has lowered the average age of residents and added more rentals to its housing stock, but it has not attracted the families of large international corporations. For example, few international executives at Volkswagen Chattanooga chose to locate their families in East Ridge. Economic class is a relatively unspoken element in the mini-cultures of the South, including East Ridge. The City's working class persona and the City's fight to maintain its economy in these hard times has not always been successful. Further, the housing stock is often older and smaller than affluent families usually prefer to own.

My own home is typical of an older Southern house. It was built on what had been rural land shortly after World War II. Designed in shotgun-style, the rooms were lined up to flow one into the other, with the master bedroom just off the kitchen so the lady of the house could roll out of bed and cook an early breakfast. The washer and dryer are located in the garage, which my husband, not unlike many Southerners, turned into a woodworking shop. A clothesline is immediately available in the backyard, right next to a huge storage shed. Or at least it was until a tornado felled trees and wiped out both the clothesline and the shed.

The family room is paneled in old-fashioned pinewood, which must have been a major upgrade at the time. There is a gun rack over the door to the room where the previous owner kept his rifle. The closets were miniscule, if they existed at all. There is no front-hall closet; for that matter, there is no front hall or vestibule when you enter. An old-fashioned coat rack still stands at the front door, holding our coats, not far from the old-fashioned umbrella holder. Electricity-powered heating grates were embedded in the walls of each room before we remodeled. Southern-style, we kept the grate in the family room and installed a propane tank in the backyard to provide our heat in case of emergencies. Not-so-Southern-style, we removed the hall connecting the master bedroom and the kitchen and built a walk-in closet in its place. Remodeling here is passionate, more like a sport than a hobby, and very often, it's a career path handed down through generations.

All this passion for self-reliance, for maintaining history, for independence and identity is replicated in small communities throughout the South. Many of them do not want to be labeled "Southern" because the term is too broad. That includes my colleague Anne, who lives in the Appalachian Mountains, an historic area of resources such as coal, timber, iron ore, and minerals. It's also a unique culture with British roots, but it has evolved into a distinctive American culture. Some call it "Country" and some, less kind, call it "redneck," "cracker," and "hillbilly." Anne prefers to be called just "Appalachian." And while outsiders may see Appalachia and Southern as interchangeable, that's not how it looks to the insider.

A visit to my college roommate, Linda in East Prestonsburg, Kentucky, had given me a sense of what Anne meant. At the foot of the Appalachian Mountains, the area was dotted with small farms and old farmhouses like the one Linda and her husband David had. Early one morning, I tiptoed out the unlocked door while they were asleep, crossed the one-lane road, and promptly found myself surrounded by half a dozen grazing cows. Not knowing any better, I just stood and watched, not realizing that the cows would ignore me, bump into me, and crowd me as they chewed the grass. Terrified, I escaped the closing circle of oblivious cows and poured out my shock to my hosts. They just looked at me pityingly as they munched on vegetables from their garden. Linda sighed, "When you live here, you understand how stupid cows are and you don't just stand there like that." Humbled, I contemplated the apparent gaps in my Ivy League education as we drove to Berea College where I was to teach a course in English country dance.

Berea College serves mainly Southern Appalachia, and it's here where the enormity of the different mindsets truly began to sink in. My work with country dances had a context of the formal society of lawyers, London circa 1660. The context for them in Berea was down-home folks and mountain men, probably the same ones featured in the town's Hillbilly Days celebration in the spring. Today, the dance music was not played by a classical violin, but by a couple of rough fiddles better suited to the clogging in the next room. No smooth academic re-enactment here; the smiling faces and square dance-style whirling couples matched the sounds of clogging in the next room. This was English dance no longer. It is Appalachian and I see why my colleague wants it acknowledged, honored, and preserved.

My friend Diane from Baton Rouge, Louisiana appears to have nothing in common with my Appalachian connection except for discomfort with the application of the term "Southern." She didn't reject the term outright—she's very polite—but she firmly steered towards saying "The Deep South." And then she doubled down on that by adding that Louisiana, especially the Southern part of the state, is described best as the Deep, Deep South. When I asked why, she gave me history lesson on the area, how it had been

French, had its own flag and language, separate from the rest of the South. Besides, the New Orleans area was on the Gulf (of Mexico) and, to her, that implied a culture all to itself. All you had to do to understand their uniqueness was to sample the Cajun food, listen to the Zydeco music, attend Mardi Gras, and drink a "Hurricane" in a bar in New Orleans' historic district. So, Deep, Deep South it is!

Obviously, the Southern mini-cultures don't want to be tossed willy-nilly into an overarching definition of the South. Yet, make no mistake about it, there are some things in common. There is a pride of place, of family connections, and generational continuity. The identification with local history and geography is passionate and knowing how to cook the local cuisine is almost as universal as the ability to sing the local music, or at least hum along really well. There is comfort in the familiar; wariness of the stranger. The rural roots lurk just below the surface and old-fashioned manners just above it. And floating on the surface is a shared sense of isolation where culture, history, and tradition are preserved.

Of course, not every long-time Southerner fits the traditional mold. Some long for adventure and leave the region. They may take jobs elsewhere, go to college away from home, join the military and be stationed overseas, or marry and move away. Many never return, but quite a few do come back home often to be with family. These are the Southerners who straddle the traditional and the unconventional; they move between worlds. They are often the Big Picture Folks and we'll take a closer look at them in the next chapter.

**7 TIPS FOR WORKING WITH TRADITIONALS**

1. The South is hierarchical when it comes to age. Use respectful language to your elders and to those in positions of power. Do not be insulted if younger people and/or employees address you as "sir" or "ma'am."
2. Do not assume that because Southerners are friendly that they trust you. You will have to earn that trust and be careful not to be impatient in the process. Mirror their behavior just as you would learn a foreign language.
3. Be prepared for pockets of unique cultures in the Southeast. Do not make assumptions about Southern culture and apply them universally.
4. Ask Southerners where they're from. The answer will provide considerable information about the cultural context in which they operate.
5. Ask Southerners how long they've lived here. Again, the answer provides valuable information, including major interruptions in their residency in the region.
6. If you choose to live in a traditional neighborhood, understand that you may encounter an outdoors lifestyle: dogs kept outside, porches hosting a wide variety of social life, gardens and vegetable plots, carports rather

than garages, and possibly pick-up trucks and campers in the driveways.

7. Many New Southerners who move into a traditional neighborhood wonder how to meet the neighbors. Most will wave when they see you, even when they're driving by in their cars. Wave back. A conversation isn't necessary to acknowledge them, but the wave does not imply a relationship. If you want to get to know a neighbor better and they haven't introduced themselves, go and introduce yourself. Have that conversation. They may be waiting for you, the stranger, to make the first move. Alternatively, have an open house and let the curious check you out informally.

## Chapter 9: *The Faithful*

There are few more predictable questions asked of a New Southerner than "Where do you go to church?" The number of churches in any given neighborhood and the diversity of options for churchgoers are often as surprising to non-Southern Americans as it is to the Internationals coming into the South. Understanding Southern religion in the abstract is far different from the experience on the ground. The depth of Christian identity in the South should not be underestimated, nor should the sense of a personal connection to Jesus. Respect for the Southern Christian experience is vital to success here. This is true for the unaffiliated, the casual churchgoer, the agnostic/atheist, and the wide range of non-Christian faiths that now populate the South.

Many of my trainees have been offended by this question of church affiliation. They see their faith as a personal and private activity, hardly a matter of discussion with people whom they've only just met. Further, they find it challenging to deal with a constant barrage of public prayers in the name of Jesus. Even more difficult for them is the active recruitment of many, particularly through fliers and brochures. The door-to-door witnessing, the parking lot fliers on the windshield, and the brochures laid out in public bathrooms look like cult solicitations. Some New Southerner trainees have lost their tempers, shut out neighbors, and withdrawn their children from certain schools over religion-based issues.

As the South develops increasingly into a global village, and the diversity of religious beliefs grows exponentially, it is perhaps inevitable that cultural clashes over religion multiply. Legal challenges to public prayer, particularly in the name of Jesus, are increasing nationwide, but are a major issue in the South. Many of the controversial lawsuits originate from outside of the region. These lawsuits seek a more balanced approach to church-state separation. Here in the South, that balanced approach is likely to be seen as enforcing a "Naked Public Square," a term signifying rejection of all religion and faith.

The vacuum of nothingness is seen more a symbol of invasive secularism than an accommodation of religious diversity and belief. Pick up any local newspaper in which a challenge to religious prayer is discussed before a public meeting, whether it is in a municipal venue or the chamber of commerce, and you will see the lack of interest in the separation of church and state as a logical and legal argument. Rather, the local Christian community will view the lawsuit as a threat to religious freedom, a ban on what has always been done. Here in the South, tradition and "we've always done it that way" are more persuasive to most than the legal fine print. It should come as no surprise that the growing focus of outside groups pressing for separation of church and state in the South is seen as modern-day carpetbaggers by many.

In a business context, it is essential to have respect for Christianity if you want to be successful in the South. A key element of that respect is the understanding of the variety of Christian expressions of faith in the region. The majority of Christian followers are Protestant, often Baptist, with a broad range of historical influences. The Pew Forum on Religion and Public Life classifies Protestant denominations as either 1) Mainline churches 2) Evangelical churches 3) Black Churches. Understand that for many, the underlying differences come from biblical interpretation. Fundamentalists are literal in how they understand the Bible. Evangelicals are literalists, but may also heavily focus on sharing, which will appear as proselytizing to many, but their "born-again" emphasis is deeply ingrained in the faith. Mainline churches, including Methodist, Episcopal, Presbyterian, and Lutheran traditions may vary in the interpretation of scripture, but are often viewed as more liberal.

Sorting out who's who will probably be beyond the New Southerner. Many Christian churches fall into more than one category. The Pew Forum lists more than 28 Protestant traditions, with many of the names, such as "Free Methodist Church" sounding as if it belonged in one category, Mainline in this case, but in fact, belonging in the Evangelical category. The list also includes a few traditions that refer to a regional or local identity: The Lutheran Missouri Synod and The Church of God of Cleveland, Tennessee. It's not surprising that the regional designations in the Pew Forum are in Southern or Southern-border states. The Good Lord may be everywhere, but in the South, all religion is local.

Thus the Southern question: "Where do you go to church?" The answer not only indicates your belief system, but immediately identifies who you know, who you're related to, and where you'll most likely be on holy days. Your questioner will know, or will think they know, what religious music you hum, who you vote for, and what charities you support. To respond to the question that you have no religious affiliation and don't intend to have one is to create confusion. You will create an emotional response that can quickly progress from disorientation to disappointment to resentment to unforgiving hostility. The level of emotion depends on your body language and tone of voice. If you smile and have an empathetic tone, the emotional response will be tolerable. If your expression is angry and your tone aggressive or defensive, the response may be quite hostile, even though their upbringing dictates a polite reaction.

As a Jew, I am well aware that the social marker of religious affiliation extends well beyond Christianity. I'm asked which synagogue I attend, followed by questions about the people I know in the congregation. My name is a common one in the Jewish community so I'm asked if I'm related to others with the same last name. I leave theology alone. I keep to this policy even when asked if I identify with the local Messianic Jewish organization by simply explaining that despite the terminology, they are Christian and I am not. It's a distressing situation for the Jewish community, but with the limited exposure to Judaism in the South, confusion with these Messianic groups that practice ancient Hebrew traditions is not uncommon.

While religious diversity is growing in the South, few non-Christian traditions are as well known as Judaism. Jews migrated to the South early in its history with a community in Charleston, South Carolina since 1695. By 1800, Charleston was the largest Jewish community in America. My visit to the cemetery associated with K.K. Beth Elohim, one of the oldest synagogues in America, was eye opening in the extent of Jewish life and contribution to the city. By 1861, one-third of all Jews in America lived in Louisiana. According to Thomas C. Mandes,
writing for the *Washington Times* in 2002, the largest ethnic group to serve the Confederacy, was Jewish. Mandes notes that the more than 10,000 Jews who fought for the Confederacy fought not for slavery, but for states' rights, free trade, and freedom from what was seen as Northern intimidation.

Despite the long history of Jews in the South, only a small percentage of American Jews live in the region (not counting Florida). According to Dr. Stuart Rockoff, Director of History at the Institute of Southern Jewish Life, less than 10% of American Jews are in the South. Often migrating to the South to set up retail stores, as my great grandfather had done in Bermuda, Jewish shop keepers settled in numerous small Southern cities. Dr. Rockoff reports that local newspapers would celebrate the arrival of Jewish merchants as a sign that of economic growth. The Jewish newcomers were often civic leaders with 200 of them serving as city mayors since the Civil War. Chattanooga' newly elected Jewish mayor, Andy Berke, may seem like an historic first, but he is the city's third Jewish mayor. He follows in the footsteps of George Washington Ochs-Oaks (brother of Adolph Ochs) and Joseph Wasserman more than a century ago.

The time gap represents, in part, a shift from a rural to an urban economy, the rise of chain stores, and the migration of young professionals to larger cities. The shift has meant difficult periods in the Jewish community. The 1913 lynching of a Jewish factory supervisor from New York City, Leo Franke, accused of killing a 13-year factory worker from a rural family, was a perfect storm of regional, religious, and economic conflict and dislocation. Such violence has not re-occurred and today, intense curiosity is the most common response to my Jewishness.

The social and economic trends did, however, have far-reaching impact on many smaller Jewish communities. Population shifts meant that many of them virtually disappeared. Larger Jewish communities continue to change with the times. Memphis' large Jewish population is shrinking; Nashville's Jewish community is growing. Some college towns are hosting a new influx of Jewish students and faculty including Auburn and Tuscaloosa in Alabama, Knoxville in Tennessee. The influx of Jews from outside of the South is growing some metropolitan areas; Atlanta's Jewish population is about 120,000, breaking all historical records. Most Jews are relatively comfortable in the South, even as they are theologically quite distinct from the majority.

I received an e-mail from a pastor who had heard that I was writing about religion in the South. He commended me on my courage and shared stories how as a boy in Alabama, his friends had continually beaten up the Jewish kids in the neighborhood. When he asked why they kept doing it, the response was, "Because the Jews killed Christ." I asked Dr. Rockoff his thoughts on this issue and he responded by reminding me that this view is not limited to the South. It's true that I was accused of murder as a girl in Bermuda and again in public school in New York. It's also true that acceptance was easier by embracing the differences with a smile, willingly assume the teaching role as needed, and choosing battles carefully, very carefully. But it came as no surprise that many Southern Jews are advocates for inclusion and many joined the Civil Rights Movement with considerable passion.

One of the memorable Jewish leaders in the collaboration for Civil rights was Ruth Holmberg, publisher emeritus of *The Chattanooga Times Free Press*. Holmberg is a member of the family that founded the newspaper, a former director of *The Associated Press* and *The New York Times* Company, a former president of the Chattanooga Area Chamber of Commerce and of the Southern Newspaper Publisher Association, and Tennessee Woman of the Year in 2003. She is a board member of the Public Education Network, which she helped create. The historical synagogue, Mizpah Congregation, in Chattanooga Tennessee, continues in large part due to her support.

The first time I had the opportunity to meet Ruth Holmberg was at a meeting for the Black-Jewish Coalition held at the Urban League's Chattanooga headquarters. She has been an advocate for civil rights since the beginning of the movement. In interviews, Holmberg described segregation in Chattanooga when she arrived in late 1946. She talked about the colored water fountains and the restricted restaurants and hotels. "I had to arrange a workshop for music critics and the African American music critic from Detroit couldn't stay in the Reed House with the other critics." In 1954, *The Chattanooga Times* supported the Supreme Court's famous desegregation case, *Brown vs. the Board of*

*Education.* Argued by then NAACP attorney, Thurgood Marshall, the Supreme Court ruled unanimously that the "separate but equal" doctrine was unconstitutional, laying the foundation for ending segregation of students based on their skin color. Chattanooga did not see the ensuing violence that other Southern cities experienced. However, the newspaper did lose circulation and received threatening phone calls. Holmberg was neither intimidated nor deterred from supporting civil rights and quality education for all students.

One of my favorite projects in those early years as Executive Director of the Jewish Federation was a Black-Jewish arts celebration for schoolchildren hosted at the Bessie Smith Cultural Center. Planning the event with the Black-Jewish Coalition, particularly LaFonde McGee, I formed life-long friendships. We were thrilled when a dozen school buses arrived with public school students for an unprecedented cross-cultural field trip of music, poetry, and dance. However, I'm sorry to report that today, the Black-Jewish field trip no longer exists, nor does the Black-Jewish Coalition. Attrition and economics eroded the coalition and its projects. Those writing the history of Black- Jewish relations will point out the complexities of the relationship, the motivations, and the stressors. Historians will include the formidable personalities who were involved and underscore how all religious connections go deep in the South. The New Southerner should look at the full picture in order to understand religion here: the personalities, generations, politics, economics, and, most definitely, history.

Bringing the Black churches in the South into focus cannot be done without reference to slavery and Civil Rights. According to the official website of the AME Church (African Methodist Episcopal), the Church originated out of a freed-slave civic society in Philadelphia in the early 1880s, giving African Americans a place to worship that was often closed to them in white churches. After the Civil War, the AME church expanded into the South and by 1880, membership had reached 400,000. Many churches in the South continue to this day to be separated into predominantly Black or White congregations. Many Black churches maintain an ongoing Civil Rights orientation. And while there is an historic racial divide among Southern churches, the depth of Christian identity spans racial differences. However, expression of that faith in the Black Church can be very distinctive.

I am often asked by Internationals and New Southerners where they can go to experience the services in a Black Church. They want to experience firsthand the music of the worship services and the preaching style. They are eager for an invitation to go to a service at a Black Baptist Church. They are intrigued in particular by the Pentecostal churches in the Black community, including the Assemblies of God, the Church of God in Christ, the United Pentecostal Church International, and the

Assemblies of the Lord Jesus Christ. These churches are heavily spiritual, with lively music and worship and, their hallmark, speaking in tongues. In a blog called "Intersections," the Black Pentecostal service is described in loving detail:

> *Shouting:* And by shouting, I mean running down the aisles, dancing with abandon, jumping up and down, and of course, actually shouting. It is a spontaneous joyful response to God in worship; and expression of being touched by the Spirit. You could run, jump, yell, fall out on the floor, and it was contagious. If one rejoiced, others would join in – jumping feet first into the flow of the Spirit and allow themselves to be carried away.

While the Protestant churches dominate Christianity in the South, there has long been a substantial Catholic presence with four archdiocesan headquarters in the region today. The Roman Catholic Archdiocese of New Orleans is the second-oldest diocese in the present-day United States, having been elevated to the rank of diocese in 1793. The Roman Catholic Archdiocese of Louisville was established in 1808 and it now comprises the states of Kentucky and Tennessee. The Archdiocese of Mobile established in 1825 includes Alabama and Mississippi. The Archdiocese of Savannah was established in 1850, expanded in the Savannah/Atlanta Archdiocese, which morphed into the Atlanta

Archdiocese in the 1930s as Catholic demographics changed, now covering Georgia, and North and South Carolina.

The Roman Catholic Church divides the US into 14 regions. When you combine the growth in Hispanic membership in Alabama, Kentucky, Louisiana, Mississippi, and Tennessee (Region 5) with Georgia, and North and South Carolina (Region 14), the South has the highest percentage increase in Hispanic Roman Catholics than any other regions in the United States: 117%.

The influx of Internationals is not unique to the Catholic Church. Many of the older, established religious institutions in the South are affected.
This is no surprise to Southerners who only have to drive around town to see the international impact. Secondary signs frequently swing from church doors, announcing services for Filipinos, Latinos, and Koreans. Check out the websites of dioceses in the region and you will find links to Hispanic Ministries, a sign of the times and of things to come.

The Internationals are also impacting institutional affiliations among non-Christians. They also will be asked, "What church do you attend?" The term "church" is a catch-all idiom for all religious institutions, although that is changing as synagogues, temples, and mosques become more common. There are Bahai communities throughout the South. The number of

Hindu temples is growing: two in Alabama, nine in Georgia, four in Louisiana, three in Mississippi, five in North Carolina, three in South Carolina, four in Tennessee, five in Virginia, and one in West Virginia.

Other groups are less prominent in numbers, but nonetheless have a Southern presence. The World Buddhist Directory shows 11 Buddhist organizations in Alabama, 50 in North Carolina, 41 in Georgia, 16 in Louisiana, six in Mississippi, 11 in South Carolina, 28 in Tennessee, 49 in Virginia, and seven in West Virginia. There are also established Jain groups in Georgia, Tennessee, South Carolina, and West Virginia.

In general, the quiet growth and changes in the religion arena of the South has generated little controversy. However, that has not been the case with one group, the mosque in Murfreesboro, Tennessee. It is not as if this is the first and only mosque built in the South. Georgia is ninth in the country for the number of mosques (69) in the state and Atlanta, Georgia is the 8th largest metropolitan area in the US for its number of mosques. There are 27 mosques in Louisiana, 38 in TN, 62 in Virginia, 21 in South Carolina, 16 in Mississippi, 50 in North Carolina, and seven in West Virginia. But this mosque, in this place, at this time, generated a firestorm that has gone on for years.

The controversy began about the same time as the controversy surrounding the mosque built near Ground Zero in New York City. The sense of being threatened created a huge protest movement against the building of this mosque. Court cases were brought against the Muslim community with the intent of disbanding attempts to build. The rhetoric was heated and ugly, but while the building efforts were delayed, the mosque eventually did open. A mosque in Chattanooga, Tennessee was inaugurated not long after the Murfreesboro building. The opening was uneventful and was attended by Jews and Christians as well as Muslims. A photo of me and the rabbi from my synagogue, Mizpah Congregation, appeared on their site as guests attending the opening celebration.

Despite our determination to avoid any resemblance to the Murfreesboro situation, interfaith work in the South is limited. Coalitions are frequently more ecumenical than interfaith in nature; involving diverse Christian groups. However, good works do provide an exception to this rule and you will find a diversity of religious groups involved in community projects. Most recently, the tornadoes that devastated wide swaths of the South were a call to all people of faith to help others, regardless of affiliation. When I signed up with the City of East Ridge for assistance in clearing away the devastation around our home, a contingent of Mormon volunteers appeared at my doorstep. Faith in the purpose of charity and kindness to those in need far outweighed any other consideration.

The sense of divine presence among Southerners is powerful and enduring. If there is religious conflict, resolution rarely includes removal of all religious references. Public schools are primary targets. Local newspapers run front-page stories of reigning cheerleaders who use biblical verses, football coaches who have Christian prayers before a game, and public school graduation ceremonies in churches. Programs that relied on churches to provide buses to take public school students on field trips are increasingly shut down. Resentment of the removal of religious references and partnerships runs deep among many Southerners.

What does all this mean for your children in Southern public schools? Issues of religious songs and symbols are usually addressed quietly. Negotiations for children of non-Christian families take place behind closed doors. These students are often excused from assemblies where they would feel uncomfortable. Others will simply go with the flow. For them, Christmas trees are secular holiday symbols, as are the red and green lights, boughs of holly, and flying sleighs, and reindeer. Their homes don't sport any of this secular/Christmas paraphernalia and they are well aware of the cultural divide. However, unless you are willing and able to go to war, the Christian secular symbols of Christmas are generally agreed to be relatively harmless.

Some may feel that private schools will be more accommodating of religious differences. This is not always the case. When prayer and chapel are part of the required curriculum, students who do not comply may be invited to find alternative schooling. Yes, there have been incidences of non-Southern families who object to the prayer requirements of private schools being asked to remove their child. Southerners understand the unwavering commitment beforehand and plan accordingly. New Southerners need to match their expectations to reality for a productive, comfortable life in the South. Understanding the religious context is a major component of that process.

## 5 TIPS FOR NEW SOUTHERNERS

1. When asked, "What church do you belong to?" consider the context. If you want or need a relationship with the questioner, do not be curt, dismissive, or rude.
2. If you would like to visit a church, have someone invite you along. It's the easiest way to feel welcome there.
3. Be aware that objecting to public prayers making reference to Jesus may be a logical extension of church-state separation to you, but can appear threatening to many. Choose your battles wisely.
4. New Southerners would be wise to follow the old adage, "Don't discuss religion or politics." The two are closely aligned in the South with a long and complex history that can render off-hand remarks easily offensive. Don't be in a hurry to critique religion and religious issues.
5. Southerners should understand that religious affiliation is highly personal to many Newcomers. Be aware that asking about their church membership may make them feel uncomfortable, and possibly insulted.

## Chapter 10: *The Icons: Who's Trending & Why You Should Follow*

I sat in a Southern college auditorium featuring an annual Asian conference and listened to professors and trade experts talk about trends in international relations. A member of the audience asked, "What does Asia know about the South?" The expert answered by listing several Southern icons. The first on the list, predictably, was "Elvis." In all my years of travel, teaching, and training, I have never met a blank stare at the mention of Elvis. Many have either visited his home, Graceland, or plan on visiting. Occasionally, I come across an international executive who breaks into an Elvis song, telling a story as Southern songs do, with perfect English, a Southern accent, and a couple of Elvis' hip actions. Elvis will never completely "leave the building."

The second item on the Southern icon list was "country music." Music has been one of the South's most successful exports, fueling national and global entertainment enterprises. Music is also a major tool for crossing cultural boundaries. When clients from Eastern Europe tell me that they love country music, they're well on their way to being comfortable in the South.

Defining Southern music is challenging because it includes an almost limitless variety of styles. There's

Blues, Rhythm & Blues, Bluegrass, Gospel, Rockabilly, and Zydeco, just to name a few. The Asian expert didn't offer details of which country music he meant, but as a gentleman from a longtime White Southern family, it's very likely that he meant the traditional country music. With minimal accompaniment, usually string instruments, cowboy, mountain, and "hillbilly" music gained popularity around 1910, along with the radio.

The genre became so popular that many early country singers capitalizing on the trend had no roots anywhere resembling "country." Early country music is often dated from the music of the Carter Family from Virginia and the Appalachian Mountains. If you don't know their Celtic-flavored songs, including "Keep on the Sunny Side of Life (1928)," you might know the next generation, June Carter, and her famous song, "Ring of Fire." And if you don't June, you might know and should know the husband who joined her in singing "Ring of Fire," Johnny Cash.

There are generations of country music stars from the South. Follow any and all of them; there are musical gems galore. If you're a stickler for details, you can browse through the many sites that track the generations and the genres in different ways, with many names appearing in different categories at the same time. Some of the sites will direct you to country singers who sang mountain-style songs, including Loretta Lynn, Roy Clark, and Porter Wagoner. Others will send you to the banjo-playing style of bluegrass with stars like Earl

Scruggs and Ricky Skaggs. You may already be familiar with contemporary country singers like Garth Brooks, Faith Hill, Shania Twain, and *American Idol* stars, Scott McCreery and Carrie Underwood. Our graying speaker could have been referring to any of them, but he didn't give names and no one asked. Just the mention of international recognition of country music international was enough to get the audience hooting and clapping and whistling. That's the kind of attention a New Southerner can get by mentioning a love of country music. As for local students wanting to go into international work, I advise them to learn some country favorites and be ready to sing them at a moment's notice, but don't pretend to be a country singer.

Country musicians often looked like folks who wandered into stardom by pure dumb luck. Accessible, attainable, and populist, Southern music seemed effortless and spontaneous. The image of random, unpredictable success was nurtured and promoted by artists and sharp business people alike. The legends of rags to riches were woven into the music, into the industry created around it, and into the country music capital of Nashville, Tennessee. The image of authentic, down-to-earth folks with a hint of childlike innocence became an enduring Southern mascot of sorts. Follow the series *Honey Boo Boo* to see the image played out on television today.

Rags, riches, and dumb luck were a major element in the commercialization of the cult movie *O Brother, Where art*

*Thou?* The movie is the odyssey of a couple of losers who become overnight music sensations during the Depression. They sing on a primitive, scratchy recording at a radio station in the middle of Southern nowhere. With the radio newly invented, they journey through poverty, crime, floods, scams, violence, racism, marital strife, and political campaigns culminating in a standing ovation onstage. The music sequences are mesmerizing, combining the poor Old South with Hollywood's latest technology disguised as a grainy, black and white film. What a package!

The genius of the movie includes George Clooney, the A-List star known for his slick performances. Clooney appears in overalls, hankering after Dapper Dan hair gel, dreaming big, and specializing in what some folks might call 'lying.' The against-type character is sure to get our attention. But wait! Publicists tell us that Clooney started out as a movie extra in his hometown Augusta, Kentucky. Another rags-to-riches legend is born and commercialized. We follow Clooney as an American icon, but not necessarily his Southern roots.

Why not? The South may provide a romantic, dramatic, and creative backdrop, but it also comes with baggage that doesn't necessarily translate outside the region. Augusta, Kentucky is a good example of the push and pull of Southern icons. The city's website asserts that it was a major inspiration for the Kentucky state song, "My Old Kentucky Home." The song's creator, Stephen Foster (1826-1824), is often called "America's First

Composer." Foster's "parlor songs" for intimate gatherings remain famous for their gentle, sentimental beauty, including "Beautiful Dreamer."

Foster also wrote for minstrel shows, trying to upgrade the content of the vaudeville-like performances done by white men in "blackface." When I asked Northerners their opinion on "My Old Kentucky Home," the response was that it was "racist." It does not resonate well with many non-Southerners, nor does the entire minstrel tradition, considered today as racist and demeaning with negative stereotyping outweighing any entertainment and/or artistic value. Foster's minstrel songs became food for the satire of the 1974 movie *Blazing Saddles*. When the white cowboys urge the former slaves to sing, they're outraged by the smooth rendition of "I Get No Kick from Champagne," composed by one of America's most urbane Broadway songwriters, Cole Porter (1891-64). The cowboys then demonstrate how the former slaves should sing by breaking into Foster's "Camptown Ladies," jumping, leaping, a-hootin' and a-hollerin' to the refrain, "The Camptown Ladies sing this song, Doo-dah, Doo-dah, The Camptown racetrack's five miles long, Oh, de-doo-dah- day ..."

Foster was a Northerner who empathized with the situation of black men; he only traveled through the South once, but successfully used the region's colorful scenes and history in his work. I doubt he ever imagined that his songs would be in the public eye more than a century later. If he had, I like to imagine that he'd have deleted references to "Mammy," "darkies," and his "longing for de old plantation." The terms appear in "The Swanee River (Old Folks at Home)," which was Florida's state song until 2007, when the state could no longer support the historic, but now-racist, language. Foster lived in a transitional age when styles were changing, pre-civil war images resonated, and songwriter as a career didn't exist. Struggling to make a living, Foster died alone and broke in New York City at the age of thirty-seven. Music, and Southern music, is light years away from Foster's era, but the issues of language and popular appeal have not gone away.

With the Black and White cultures so divided in the South and throughout the U.S., iconic figures developed separately. The South gave birth to some of the most memorable and glorious African American female vocalists from the South: Jazz singer Ella Fitzgerald (b. Newport News, Virginia 1917-1996), Gospel great, Mahalia Jackson: (b. New Orleans, LA (1911-1972) and Queens of Soul music: Gladys Knight (b. Atlanta, GA 1944...) and Aretha Franklin (b. Memphis TN 1942 ...) As memorable, if not more so, as the female vocalists were the African American men, who were the trendsetters in their genres. You should know the names of jazz artists Louis Armstrong (b. New Orleans 1901-1971) and John Coltrane (b. Hamlet, North Carolina 1926-1967), R & B (Rhythm & Blues) artist Ray Charles (b. Albany, GA 1930-2004) and Rock icons like Little Richard (b. Macon, GA 1932 ...), James Brown (b.

Barnwell, S. Carolina 1933 -2006), and Chuck Berry (b. St. Louis Missouri 1926…).

The influence of these African American musicians spread not only throughout the U.S., but into Europe. Muddy Waters may have been born in Mississippi (1913- 1983) but his music launched the Chicago blues. Yet, it wasn't just Chicago that resonated to his deep-voiced, southern-style blues. He inspired Mick Jagger and the Rolling Stones, and numerous British musicians to affect a southern bluesy sound in the sixties and beyond. Check out the video on Youtube of Muddy Waters and the Rolling Stones singing "Hoochie Coochie Man" in 1981. While you're in the mood, check out a few concert videos by Usher (Origin Chattanooga, TN 1978 …) and see how the music and the industry have grown, evolved, and continue to impact globally.

The appeal of the Southern, African-American music internationally was underscored in the 1991 cult-favorite movie called *The Commitments*. It features an odd assortment of white, working-class teens in Dublin, Ireland, who are driven by the seemingly universal urge to put a band together, perform, and aim for glory. The interplay of Irish and Southern accents with earthy, irreverent humor is a comical display of culture clash. The most memorable moment for me was when one of these Irish band members announces, "I'm Black, and I'm proud!" You will laugh at the absurdity; you will cry that the band argues and falls apart. You will be pleased to know that the band does reunion tours occasionally.

Music is a major tool for crossing cultural boundaries whether Southern, American, or International. However, be aware and sensitive to the fact that white-dominated music companies have been accused of co-opting Black music. Many white artists gained commercial success borrowing from Black music while the African-American originators remained in relative obscurity. Even Elvis' successful combination of hillbilly and blues can be viewed in this light. Yet, despite the complex history, when an international executive in the South tells me that they love Southern music, I know that they've begun to acculturate. Whether they mean Elvis, Usher, or, as often happens, the fictitious Hannah Montana, Southern music is becoming part of them.

As I sway to "The Wish" by Rascal Flatts and do some toe-tapping to "Fishin' in the Dark" by The Nitty Gritty Dirt Band, I'm reminded that music made up only two-thirds of the icons listed by our university speaker. He had one more item that resonated across the globe, and that was golf. It appears that when doing business in Asia, particularly Japan, golf is a frequent topic and activity. According to Earl Berkun, a former design engineer of golf equipment, golf has been a favorite sport in Japan for decades. He describes the passion for golf in business circles, and how it is a status symbol for executives to be on the golf course, given the 50-60 hour work week. Many executives keep their golf clubs in their office, easily visible to all who enter. Japanese companies have bought golf courses in the South and throughout the U.S. because land is more plentiful and less expensive here in America. Yet, despite some excellent golf courses and tournaments like the one in Augusta, Georgia, golf is not the signature sport of Southerners.

Yes, some play golf and tennis, some ride horses, hunt, fish, swim, and bowl. But to see the most popular sports in the South, I go to the high school track on a sunny afternoon in my small Southern town of East Ridge. The East Ridge High School track actually has three levels. On one level, there are two Hispanic soccer teams playing in their uniforms with family and friends cheering them on. On the other side of Level 1, the school's softball team is having a practice session. The ROTC is practicing its marching maneuvers on the field between the two sides until it can take over the gym, where the basketball team is finishing its game.

On the second level, there are students running intervals and team relays. In the center of the track, the young men are practicing for an upcoming high school football game. The sound of the coach's voice shouting directions carries up to the next level, where a group of cheerleaders is practicing for the big game. As their cheers fade, the field is taken over by peewee football practice. Five- and six-year-olds take turns running and tackling each other like frisky puppies with intent faces. One of the kindergarteners runs with the ball, gets tackled from behind, and falls to the ground with his arms wrapped around the ball like a pro.

New Southerners who like to play sports can chose any or all of the above and make friends quickly. If you don't play a sport, be an enthusiastic spectator. NASCAR has Southern roots and maintains racetracks in states throughout the Southeast. (NASCAR stands for "National Association for Stock Car Auto Racing.") NASCAR has become so popular that tracks are being built outside the South. According to *Sports Illustrated* (Estes, SI.com), the historically Southern drivers from Alabama, Georgia, South Carolina, Tennessee, and Kentucky are being edged out by non-Southerners. New fans will be greatly appreciated and you can toast the winner with Jack Daniels or a coke The coke refers to almost any kind of soda and the Jack Daniels is iconic Southern whiskey. As one friend says, "As long as you have a Jack Daniels in one hand and a coke in the other, you just can't lose." Not into racecars? Watch football games of any kind: high school, college, or professional. Watch them on television and attend the games. If you are fortunate enough to get an invitation to watch a football game with a group of friends, accept and go. If it's a Super Bowl party, go and be prepared to eat nonstop. Don't bother to count calories; the Southern cooking at these parties is geared toward celebration and indulgence.

Spectators are often on the golf course, regardless of whether they actually play the game, to watch tournaments. Every April, my family follows the most celebrated of golf tournaments in the South, in Augusta, Georgia. Created in the 1930s, The Masters is one of the four major championships in professional golf and is played every year at the Augusta National Golf Club. Famous for attracting big-name competitors from around the country and the world, The Masters also can be a sports soap opera. The news seems to be as much about the lives of the players, their wives, and ex-wives, as it is about their plays. We follow The Masters' growing pains as it tackles its exclusive past and deal with the issue of women members. I've found that you need to know a bare minimum about the sport itself to have a lively conversation about Augusta. If you play the sport, attend The Masters, and experience a genuine cultural phenomenon as national and international fans convene for the festivities.

## 5 STRATEGIES FOR USING AND FOLLOWING ICONS:

1. Pick a Southern musician or two to follow. Personalities are key conversation pieces in the South and are a good tool for making friends.
2. Choose a Southern music genre to follow. Get familiar with the musicians in the genre. Attend a festival where the genre is featured. Festivals and concerts can be found in most locations in the South, particularly in the warm weather months.
3. If you sing or play an instrument, learn some Southern songs. The experience will give you a feel for Southern culture and give you something to share with others.
4. Follow a local sports team. Choose a sport that you like, regardless of whether you play it or not, and become a fan. If you do play a sport, join a group, team, or association where you can meet others who share your interest.
5. Know the names of the major sports teams in your state, especially college and professional football teams. Learn who their major competitors are and know the team colors. Even if you don't choose to wear the colors personally, recognize and compliment those who do.

## Chapter 11: *The Big Picture Folks: What New Southerners Bring to the Table*

A constant stream of people with a global mindset and tendency to "make no small plans" has come into the South and many more are expected in the future. The Southeast "sunbelt" saw a population increase of 32% between 1970 and 1990. The coastal counties are projected to grow another 41% between 2000 and 2025, according to a report from the US National Assessment of the Potential Consequences of Climate Variability and Change. Some Traditionalists may feel threatened by the rapid demographic changes. On several occasions, I've been asked to make sure that my work highlights the values and traditions of Southern culture. I am honored to be seen as a trustworthy bridge between the Old and the New South. And given the rapid influx of New Southerners, a bridge is definitely needed.

The Big Picture folks bring their own values and traditions, but they also bring new ideas, businesses, and opportunities. They fall into four major categories, each with their own brand of futurism: 1. Naturalized Southerners  2. Expats  3. Returning Southerners  4. American transplants. Each group enriches the region with its fresh ideas, unique perspective, and cross-cultural awareness. Working together, they are a boiling, bubbling cauldron of Big Picture innovation.

*Naturalized Southerners*

Immigrants have traditionally come to America seeking to better their economic situation. In recent years, immigrants increasingly come to the South for work in various industries: manufacturing, education, healthcare, and commerce. Some of the fastest growing international companies in the US are located in the South, including North Carolina, Georgia, Louisiana, and Tennessee, as reported by the Ewing Marion Kauffman Foundation. The Foundation also reports that the South is home to largest number of founders who started their companies locally. Southerners often don't want to relocate away from family and friends, but naturalized entrepreneurs can inspire them to expand, think locally and globally.

Alnoor Dhanani is the CEO of Double Cola, an old Southern company that Alnoor and his family bought decades ago. A polyglot of cultures, the Dhanani family was originally from Indian. Alnoor was born in East Africa where the family served as cheap labor in the British colony. He attended high school in London where his grandfather had started a general store. When the family made the decision to buy Double Cola and turn it into a worldwide export company, they delegated Alnoor to head the business. Emigrating to America, Alnoor took over the Double Cola headquarters in

Chattanooga and grew it into the national and global enterprise envisioned. Raising his children as Americans, Alnoor added to the region's assets. His son, a computer expert, established a foundation to assist young people to realize their dreams.

There were two elements of his business that Alnoor emphasized as being needed in the region. The first was the understanding that exporting products and services is the wave of the future. Without growing our exports, we will not grow our economy. The second element that he highlighted was technology, particularly for office use. According to Alnoor, while Americans are adept at using some technologies, there are nations, including many we perceive as poorer and less educated than Americans, which are ahead of us. He used the example of Bangladesh where offices were replacing fax machines with scanning devices years before most American offices made the transition.

Alnoor's determination to develop his workers as well as the business itself is evident in his personnel policies. The investment made in the staff at the headquarters includes college tuition regardless of the subject studied. He insists that productivity is enhanced by time off and vacation time is ample and paid, including expenses. Alnoor's passion for developing human capital is visible in local community projects and those in developing countries. He is at home traveling for weeks at a time to visit both customers and his projects. Ambition, entrepreneurship, global mindset, and local leadership are the Big Picture gifts of the Naturalized Southerner.

*Expats*

Internationals who come to the South temporarily add technical expertise to foreign companies, particularly those in the start-up mode. They also add global perspective that enhances the self-awareness of Southerners and adds new dimensions to the growing global mindset. Journalist Beate Ziehres came to Tennessee from Bavaria, Germany with her husband, who worked for Volkswagen Chattanooga. Like many of Volkswagen's engineers and plant operators in its early phases, Bodo Ziehres came on a multi-year contract, with plans to return home when his contribution to the start up was complete. He, Beate, and their children became Expat Southerners, immigrants who developed a perspective of the South that is helpful for the long-term development not only of Volkswagen, but of the community where it now makes its home.

Beate wrote several articles for the American Diversity Report, sharing her perspective about her foster home. In this article, Beate wrote about generosity in the face of destructive tornados in the South. Here's how she described the Southern response to Mother Nature's fury.

> I was planning on telling you about the cute lady who rescued my son's kite that was stuck in the

pillars of the Walnut Bridge over Coolidge Park in Chattanooga, TN. In my home country (Germany), nobody would have cared about a burning house or a boy with a stranded kite.

But something happened when I returned from Germany that stopped me writing and confirmed my thoughts. This was when a swarm of deadly tornadoes destroyed whole towns in the Chattanooga area. Five weeks later, the first stormy night after the catastrophe lies behind us but another record-breaking tornado raged through the Midwest of the country. And I can be sure now that there is at least one cultural difference. Lots of folks from around the Scenic City still spend time helping those in need.

I was deeply impressed by the level of helpfulness and my respect will never end. I've heard from women, men, and also teenagers who went out to the destroyed areas. They helped people they didn't know. In the first hours and days after the storm, volunteers looked for injured people or bodies, and cleared debris. Even today the wave of help hasn't subsided.

Wherever I go and to whomever I talk, the destructive force of nature that came over us is still a subject of conversation. Innumerable volunteers will have to struggle with the scenes they saw, with the experiences they had. A friend of mine who is an author of murder mystery novels gained a few ideas while walking between wooden piles which had been homes. "It's too early to write about it', she said. But she will store the impressions in her head, as so many will do, until the furor of the terrible events of April 27 have died out.

We are glad not to get tornadoes of this intensity in Germany. But if it happened, their assistance would be different. Of course, people would give money. But I can't imagine they would spend weeks helping with their own hands.

Southerners greatly appreciated the attention given to the highlighting the values and traditions of the region. These are the elements of Southern culture that Southerners want to see as permanent, translatable into a fast-moving society. At the same time, they have had to wrap their minds around perceptions of America and the South that are quite negative. The impact of the increased cultural awareness is very visible. Today, grocery stores and restaurants in the region carry more food for international tastes than ever in our history. The emphasis on technology by these companies is spurring new educational opportunities in STEM (Science, Technology, Engineering, Math). High schools, colleges, and education-oriented nonprofits are scrambling to create the global leaders, skilled workers, and international team members of the future. A sense of adventure, a passion for new experiences, and an appreciation of cultural differences are the Big Picture gifts of our Expat Southerners.

*Returning Southerners*

What about long-time Southerners who left and returned to live amongst family and friends? Deb Hunter is one such person and describes her roots in Southern history. "My father's family has been in the TN/GA area ten generations, since the area was known as the Cherokee Nation. Before that, the family was in Colonial Charleston, SC. I may be one of the most Southerner persons you will ever meet." When asked why she decided to travel elsewhere, Deb responded, "As it is for most people, I left in search of career advancements. I moved to Los Angeles with my best friend and worked for Jose Eber's hair salon while trying to make connections in the music business."

Despite the lure of California, Deb returned to the South. "I decided that Nashville was a better fit for me culturally and I like keeping a close proximity to my family. It's a personal thing." Like all returning Southerners, she came back to a region both familiar and changed and describes both. "What looks the same? The fact that you can still drive take a thirty-minute drive to a rural area from any of the metropolitan areas." Sharing what looks different, Deb immediately talks about the physical changes and the regional growth. "The first two changes that come to mind are the Nashville skyline and Atlanta traffic."

One of the biggest changes for Deb are those created by life-style decisions. "On a personal level, I live in a multi-cultural household with my Scottish-born husband. I understand the needs and concerns of the preserving the best of our past, the realities of the present, and future hopes and dreams for a prosperous new tomorrow in our beautiful region." As the former executive director of the World Chamber of Commerce based in Atlanta, Deb encouraged small businesses, corporations, entrepreneurs, and students to expand their reach worldwide. She illustrates the new global realities in her work as a writer, publishing e-books and articles online, reaching a worldwide audience. Deb travels effortlessly between a deeply Southern heritage and a futuristic Southern-global vision. The ability to have a foot in the South of the past, present, and future South is the Big Picture gift of the Returning Southerner.

*American Transplants to the South*

I sit with a handful of advisors, having breakfast at Wally's in East Ridge, discussing what we bring to the South. Few of us are originally from the region. We are from different areas in the U.S. and differ in backgrounds: ethnicity, race, gender, and religion. Except for the native Southerner, I have been here the longest, sixteen years, and am the oldest of the three generations around the table. All of us are professionals at different stages in our careers in wide array of industries: education, social work, healthcare, marketing, accounting, technology, training, event planning, and the legal profession. These are the local advisors to the American Diversity Report and Cross Cultural School of the South.

The topic of today's discussion is the changing culture in the region and the emerging business trends. Our goal is to lay out a plan for providing the cross-cultural training needed by the new Southern global village. Our view of the need has two major elements: New Southerners and those who work with them. The Internationals may be more easily identified, given the companies that are locating headquarters, offices, and plants in the region. Increasingly, they and their families are being integrated by friends and colleagues who came before them. Yes, they use acculturation services, but the need pales beside the need of the American New Southerners.

The Americans transplants come to work in the international companies, to work for their vendors, and to start new businesses serving all of the above. The transplants like those of us around the breakfast table bring valuable skills with them: technology, engineering, logistics, manufacturing, languages. Unlike some of the Internationals, we speak English and expect to acculturate to Southern culture with little stress. With time, we understand how unrealistic that expectation can be. With time, there is also understanding of what we bring to the table.

Beyond the technical know-how and professional expertise, one of the most valuable skills that transplants add to the region is planning. In a region that revolves around relationships, the objective, analytical, and goal-oriented aspects of planning can be quite foreign. One of the major factors in my being hired and brought to Chattanooga was my master's degree in urban planning & policy and the community's desire to build a new Jewish cultural center. My task was to create a path for a handful-size committee to achieve not only a building, but set in motion a generations-long initiative. Our goals were to attract newcomers, sustain long-time veterans, serve the youth, be a cultural hub for our specific community and for the community-at-large, and be a vital element in related regional, national, and international networks.

In addition to the planning strategies of goals and deadlines, transplants bring an energy that cuts across long-established patterns. Yes, they may be awkward in dealing with generational differences in the South. Internationals are often unsure how to react when employees call them "sir." They may be confused by the silence when feedback is requested. Breaking with tradition may stir controversy, but it may also fan the flames of creativity and innovation.

Gender differences in the South tend translate into traditional "Southern Gentleman" and "lady-like" manners. These manners are applicable to the workplace as well as social situations and indicate respect. A gentleman opens the door for the lady, no matter what. A lady waits for the door to be opened for her. It's unlikely that I'll see those manners and values change in my lifetime. I've grown fond of them and I'm not sure that I'd want to see them change, but I know they irritate many transplants. The influx of these impatient transplants affects women in particular.

There is a growing restlessness among Southern women, a desire for leadership, an explosion of entrepreneurship, and a determination to attain the American dream of fame and fortune. My expectations were modest when I created the Women's Council on Diversity in 2001. When I spoke on a community panel, I asked the question, "Can an intellectual women's group survive and thrive in the South?" The answer was, "Yes, but only if you're very lady-like about it." Despite reservations, the numbers of women participating increased exponentially every year. They developed into a creative think tank of New Southerners, Naturalized, Returnees, and Long-time Southerners. Collaboration and team building are the Big Picture gifts of women in the new demographics of the South.

## 7 BIG PICTURE STRATEGIES:

1. Schedule time to keep up with technological advances. Your Big Picture counterparts have probably already done so.
2. Don't dismiss Expats who are here for a short time. Pay attention to how they explore with an adventuresome spirit and learn from them. Expats, be prepared for great curiosity about everything you do, say, eat, and wear.
3. Naturalized Southerners should choose community projects from which they can benefit from social contacts and friends as well as benefit others with their skills and global mindset. Civic leaders should make community involvement easily accessible to these newcomers.
4. When dealing with traditional Southerners who emphasize relationships over all other considerations, keep your planning strategies simple at first. Be wary of combining multi-tasking with complex time lines. Learn to break up the Big Picture into small, digestible bites.
5. Transplants should seek out a few trusted fellow transplants with whom they can compare notes confidentially. The transition to the South can be stressful, but impatience and irritation can generate more resentment than compliance.
6. Women coming into the South will find many women's groups to suit their interests and needs. If

you are not inclined to join such groups, make an exception in the South.
7. Returning Southerners should take time to absorb the changes in their hometowns. Do not expect it to be as you left it and don't expect yourself to be the same person that left. Do consider how you can best apply the skills and knowledge acquired while away. Remember, you may well be the most adept cultural translator and valuable player of the Southern Big Picture.

# PART III: WHY & HOW

As you become accustomed to being in the South, you will want to navigate the culture in greater depth. We began in Part I by charting our way through the geography and history and continued our journey in Part II by exploring the people and cultural communities in the region. In Part III, we intensify the acculturation process by steering our way into the inner workings of Southern culture. The WHY & HOW of Part III will guide you through common interactions that can be confusing, unexpected, and inexplicable. Learn how to make your way through the mysteries to the journey's destination: Success in the South.

## Chapter 12: *The Social Scene: How to Be Sociable, No Matter What*

When a Southerner asks what I'm doing for Thanksgiving, I know it's not just curiosity. This is a test. Thanksgiving is Southern hospitality, culture, food, and fun all wrapped together in an appealing package that has *participate* written all over it. So I hesitate to admit that I'm having a quiet home-cooked meal at home with my husband since that will sound very much like being lost at sea. I sometimes debate saying that I've been invited to a friend's house for dinner. It isn't true, but the spirit of the answer counts more than the facts. I also consider saying that I'll be out of town having Thanksgiving with the kids. That's a perfectly respectable response. The best answer is to say that I am having everybody over to my house. This is a recipe for smooth sailing.

In the end, I "Southern" the question. By combining enthusiasm, finesse, stories, and colorful details, I demonstrate my respect for the culture and participation in its social life. I watch for unspoken signs of my success and I keep going until I get them. I do this with the added bonus of telling very few lies, or at least none that matter. "I'm cooking," I say, and then give more details when there is polite acceptance. "I've been grocery shopping for days." Now, there's more interest and I'm asked whether I'm having a big crowd or a small gathering. When I reply, "It will be a small gathering," I know enough to add, "I love to cook."

Now the facial expressions change from acceptance to happy smiles. Knowing my audience, I add a description of a recipe or two, and gain a few a bonus points. I include a few twists that I have created myself, explaining that I taught my recipe secrets to my daughter long ago. The smiles I receive in response get wider, accompanied by the soft murmurs of sweet nothings.

I was fortunate to have paid attention to headlines in the local newspaper "Holiday Fosters Togetherness, Memories" and could now navigate my way to a welcoming port. The best part of the conversation was that it was all true; I had just forgotten about cooking, holidays, and kids. I was inspired and, in twenty-four hours, my delighted husband was surrounded by a month's supply of my home-baked cookies, cupcakes, cranberry sauce, and gluten-free gravy.

Experience is vital to fully charting your course through the Southern social scene; research should be ongoing. The day before Thanksgiving, I began tracking what my Southern friends were saying on Facebook. There were numerous expressions of gratitude for divine blessings: love, family, life, and good memories. There were many thanks for the opportunity to reunite with far-flung relatives and old friends. Gatherings large and small were eagerly anticipated along with abundant food. Recipes abounded along with photos of Thanksgiving turkeys with all the fixings. And the desserts! There can't be too many desserts at Thanksgiving: banana pudding, bread pudding, pecan pie, fruit cobblers, and baked goodies packed into every corner of the house. There can't be too many people enjoying them. One of my favorite posts came from Linda, a nonprofit executive director who said, "If you're eating at my house, and I can't remember everybody I invited, be here by 1:00 p.m." Surely, the best quote from Facebook came on Thanksgiving Day: "Even my dog has a food hangover!"

When I first contemplated moving to the South, a friend and former Southerner told me, "Southern cooking is great if you don't mind getting fat." I wondered what he meant until I got here and discovered that food is central to the social scene. Everything about food is cherished here: eating, cooking, sharing recipes, and growing your own. And yes, the South has earned its reputation as the land of fattening food, laden with fat, salt, and sugar. The first thing to remember is that everything that can be fried ends up fried, including vegetables. You haven't lived until you eaten fried okra, fried green tomatoes, and green beans cooked down with fatback. Second, while not all vegetables are fattening—collard greens, turnip greens, and kale for example—the portions are huge and they're sold in bulk. When I bought just enough green beans for a single serving at a local farmer's market, the salesgirl was confused by the purchase. "What do you do with that?" she asked.

Breakfast is big enough to support a day of physical labor on a farm, even though most of us never do more than weed the garden. It is not unusual to have scrambled eggs and a breakfast meat like ham, bacon, or sausage, or a little of all three, then to have biscuits with butter and add some gravy. You can always have oatmeal, but corn lovers are truly in luck in the South. There are grits, a polenta-like corn mush, that are so iconically Southern that they are often referred to in the singular: "Grits is ..." If you're not a fan of grits, try the cornbread. So popular is the local corn bread and so revered are the cooks who make it, that there is an annual cornbread festival to celebrate and enjoy.

You can get potfuls of coffee at breakfast, but you may have to make a special request for the decaf. If you like hot tea, you can get a generic tea bag almost anywhere. Herbal teas are routine, primarily in the upscale and tourist establishments. In the summer, you can get iced tea with any meal, snack, and anything in between. Newcomers are often confused by the server's question of "sweet or unsweet" when ordering iced tea. Try the sweet tea for a true Southern experience. Sweet tea is a bit much for some folks who are not used to it, but you can always tone it down by asking for half sweet/half unsweet.

It's turkey for sure on Thanksgiving, but don't forget to sample the fried chicken, chicken-fried steak, pit barbecue, country ham, and salt pork. If your protein tastes run to seafood, then try the Jambalaya and crawfish popular in New Orleans. Barbecue is everywhere, including many backyards, the one place where the man of the house takes over cooking duties. Even if a tornado takes out your electricity for a week and falling trees flatten the shack in your back yard, there still the outdoor barbecue grill.

If you want to fit into the South, try the food, extol the food, and praise the chef. Even if you don't eat Southern, be careful about criticizing. For years, international executives coming into the area complained about the coffee. Southern entrepreneurs moved to resolve the conflict by importing European coffees in grocery stores. Coffee shops began to serve coffee geared to European tastes. Fortunately, our internationals not only frequent these shops and buy the newly provided coffee, but they bring their friends and express their thanks. Coffee as a symbol of culture clash was a lesson on all sides. Culturally aware trainees distanced themselves from the coffee-complainers. Internationals frequented the new coffee havens and were gracious in their thanks. Southerners overlooked the crass comments with their own graciousness towards those who don't know any better and entered the global economy with coffee pot in hand.

The graciousness that is the hallmark of Southern hospitality runs deep and has both beauty and duty attached to it. The beauty is its flexibility and the ability to welcome newcomers into your home in large numbers. The beauty is also in the love of family where time with relatives takes precedence over work. The duty involves manners that outsiders often describe as old-fashioned. Friendliness, at least on the surface, is taught from childhood. A smile, a please, and a thank you are minimum requirements. The norm is a hearty handshake for the newcomer, a hug for the old friend, and a compliment of kind words whenever applicable and even when they're not.

The South is a hub of social networking and relationships are solidified in person. Catch up with business contacts over working breakfasts, lunches, dinners, coffee, and receptions. The line between business associates and friends is difficult to maintain here and eventually, you give up trying to distinguish between them. You will end up going to sporting events together, as well as theater and music performances. You'll find yourself at the same fundraisers for community charities. I've conducted more business in grocery aisles and coffee shops as I've done in any office. And I've spent more time in the ladies' restroom of restaurants than you can imagine. These bathrooms are like the Grand Central Station of gossip; the gossip comes and goes at a speed faster than the Chattanooga Choo Choo ever achieved.

There is no idle gossip in the South; it's all food for thought and helpful in planning. The grapevine here is a far more efficient mode of communication than any newspaper, television story, or internet article. Pay attention and you will know who has been hired and fired, what new store is opening, and what business is coming to town long before it's made official. The downside of the gossip mill is that there are no secrets. Everyone knows everything about you and privacy is hard to come by. I explain this to trainees so that they understand that everything that they do, say, buy, and even wear will be noted. I also explain that social networking and the gossip involved bleeds over into local business practices and into local politics.

Doing business in the South requires social networking that's up close and personal. This is not an e-mail culture unless you already have a relationship. And even then, if your e-mails don't get returned, don't be surprised. Pick up the phone. Make a date to get together. If you are a cyberspace person, you're more apt to make friends through the expansiveness of Facebook than the short tweets of Twitter or the professionalism of LinkedIn. Increasingly, I have people who I don't think I've ever met come up to me and introduce themselves as one of my friends on Facebook. The correct response is, "Yes, of course! How are you?" Do not confess that you have three thousand "friends" on Facebook and have no idea who they are. Regardless of the connection, if a stranger announces that you are friends, just say "thank you." Social networking in the South does not require candor or accuracy. And bluntness is not an asset with anyone except your very closest friends and even then, please be careful.

It's the intent that counts. If someone tells me I look marvelous today, I say "thank you," even if I know that I look terrible, I'm recovering from a cold, haven't slept in two days, and forgot to put on make-up, I smile and say "thank you." While it's nice to be truthful when you give a compliment, it's not required. Southern networking runs on compliments, smiles, and invitations that may or may not be genuine. When an acquaintance says to you, "We really have to get together for lunch," the intent is to let you know that you are liked. Lunch is optional; you will get a date, time, or place if it's truly intended. Expectations that vague invitations are real are unrealistic. The good news is that there is no expiration date on the non-invitation. Work on fleshing out the relationship and that lunch date will naturally evolve.

Many New Southerners are confused by the levels of friendship and say that the initial friendliness seems like an uncomfortable mix of superficial compliments and outright lies. For those who are direct in their social dealings, there are no ambivalent issues about an invitation. Either you're invited or you're not. It takes a while for a direct New Southerner to understand that the outward friendliness is considered good manners, a required response as deeply ingrained as breathing. You are being given permission to approach further, however you are not yet extended trust and friendship, or admission into a social circle.

Newcomers need to approach friendships as if they were political campaigns. There is much glad-handing and smiling, but one cannot assume that you have that person's vote. You will need to persuade and create some confidence-building measures. There has to be some give and take, some exchange of personal information, compliments, and favors. Make a conscious effort to be neighborly, be kind, be generous, and be helpful. And as in any political campaign, half the battle is showing up.

Open any newspaper or local magazine and you will see photos of local do-gooders at a charitable function, a banquet in honor of a local celebrity or the launch of a new public initiative. There are celebrations and conventions year round, suitable for a variety of tastes: art, music, flowers, food, antique cars, pets, sports, and guns. They take place on national holidays, at annual festivals, religious holy days, school graduations, life cycle milestones, annual meetings, and seasonal festivities.

You cannot possibly attend them all, but you do need to show up periodically, if not regularly. You may not stay for the entire program, but you should make your presence known. Invited to serve on a board or committee? The answer is "yes." Can you lose track of exactly where you are, where you're supposed to be and when? You may at first; politicking on the social scene takes practice. Observe the true Southerner who has the social process down to a science. Note the meet and greet skills, note the ability to commit, but not over extend, note the skill in accommodating new people at the last moment and, above all, take note of the conversation skills applicable to virtually any situation known to mankind.

What are good topics for small talk? The weather is always a good choice. Sharing information about family works well: who's doing what and who's coming to dinner. Asking what people are doing for an upcoming holiday is a sure conversation starter. Sports, from fishing to basketball, bowling to hiking, are frequent small talk topics, particularly for the gentlemen. Combine the weather, the holiday, family, and food and you can chat all day. If you throw in the Sunday football game, you've covered Thanksgiving perfectly.

The one constant in small talk is the requirement to be upbeat. New Southerners should admire the weather, look forward to the holidays, extol their favorite foods, and share endearing stories about family. Small talk may seem up-close-and-personal, but it is also politicking at its Southern best. Say nothing negative about anyone or anything until and unless you're in company that you know well and, even then, tread lightly. Think of being on a small island where it's difficult to leave and everyone has to get along at least on a superficial level.

One of my Bermuda friends said it best: "Wonderful! Marvelous! Glorious!"

Extrovert skills and social expertise are born and bred into the Southern way of life and it's not surprising that they bleed into Southern politics. You will inevitably hear political gossip when people get used to having you around. Feel free to ask questions, but be wary of offering your opinion. Given the interlocking social circles in the South, the politician is probably a relative, friend, or friend-of-a-friend. Ask general questions about the players: What office are they running for; what district are they in; have they run for office in the past? Don't get into political analysis or partisan rhetoric until you know people well, and even then, tread lightly.

What do you do if you've made a mistake and offended someone or a group of people? If people have come to know you well, your offenses may be considered unavoidable, ingrained personality quirks. Yelling at people is offensive here as is insulting them, however casually. You might think that there were harsh consequences when my friend yelled at his guests to go get the food ordered specially for the reception, adding that if they were smart they would have figured that out already. But if you're known to be outspoken and outrageous on occasion, then it doesn't come as a surprise. The crowd will tend to just smile and go get the food, whether they wanted it or not. Obviously, the newcomer doesn't have the flexibility of the Southerner or of someone who's been here for years and has established their eccentricities. You will be expected to atone for your sins.

There are numerous atonement words woven into Southern conversations. You will lose track of the number of times you hear various softening phrases: Excuse me; please excuse; I'm sorry; I'm so sorry; I'm so very sorry; I didn't realize; I wish I'd known; Let me make it up to you; Pardon my …. (Fill in the blank). The words can be accompanied by a wide variety of body language from facial expressions of sympathy, worry, and dismay to gestures ranging from a light touch on the arm, to holding hands, to full-body hugs. The apology may follow a major faux pas such as yelling in public or a minor infraction like arriving late for a meeting. It is often indistinguishable from an expression of empathy between people who have a relationship, and indeed, that is what is intended.

Understanding the automatic nature of the apology will help the newcomer adjust to being in the South. An "excuse me" is virtually required with the invasion of personal space, regardless of the circumstance. Expect it and embrace it and you won't be upset beyond control. Don't be like one trainee who was overwhelmed at the grocery store by the constant sound of "excuse me" as shoppers got too close each other. He went berserk and crashed his cart into other customers' carts up and down every aisle in the store yelling, "Excuse me!" as he went. Note to newcomers: Hotheaded revenge is a no-no in the

South. More than a few apologies will be needed to recover if you go down that road.

Should the apologies not work and you sense that people are still wary of you, remember that compliments are highly prized in the South. The issue is not simply how sorry you are, but how important the other person is to you. An apology is not about how negligent, mistaken, and/or forgetful you are. It's about the value of the person you've offended and the value of the relationship you have together.

Relationships here take time to form and deepen from the default friendliness, but Southern humor helps the process move along. Humor, whether self-deprecating, widely exaggerated, ironic, or just plain goofy, is an art form in the South. It's frequently used in apologies, but is applied widely and enthusiastically. Observe, listen, and learn. You will be amazed, amused, and thoroughly entertained. So prevalent, so iconic is this humor and the colorful Southern sayings that embody it, that the next chapter is devoted entirely to it.

## MIZ DEBORAH'S 8 SOCIAL TIPS

1. Pay attention to the sections of the newspaper and TV news that talk about social events. You can learn who's who, what they like to attend and support, where they're likely to be, and when they'll be there.
2. Broaden your definition of "social event" to include gatherings of all kinds: charity, arts, reunions, holiday celebrations, sports, awards banquets, conventions, trade meetings and fashion shows. Understand that they are political as well as social functions.
3. Use compliments to smooth awkward moments. Practice them frequently so that they become a comfortable social tool.
4. Apologies are commonplace in the Southern culture. Accept them gracefully and offer them generously.
5. Southern cooking may not be to your taste, but don't say so. Experiment and find some dishes that suit you and don't mention the food that you dislike.
6. There are few secrets in a social environment where gossip is greatly valued. Be careful what you say, about whom, and to whom.
7. Plan your social calendar as deliberately as you would plan a project at work. Leave room for last minute developments, but choose your priorities in advance.

8. Pursue hobbies that engage you: gardening, sports, antique cars, cooking, and arts & crafts. You will be able to meet like-minded people in the multitude of associations that cater to these pursuits.

## Chapter 13: *The Southernisms: What the Colorful Sayings of the South Really Say*

Every culture has memorable sayings that are beloved by those who belong to the culture, but which may be mysterious to outsiders. Few cultures generate as many memorable phrases and as many well-loved sayings as the South. If you ask a Southerner to share a favorite local phrase, you will hear a variety of jokes, slang, and sayings. Go online to the many sites collecting Southern sayings and enjoy the earthy humor and down-to-earth wisdom. If you are a New Southerner, understand that each "Southernism" is a key to Southern culture. If you're from around here, be aware that common sayings and idioms are cultural artifacts. Putting Southernisms into their cultural context is essential for effective cross-cultural communication and that's what the purpose of this chapter.

A major cultural context is the rural roots of these sayings. While the isolated communities of early British immigrants retained the original language, they also developed a local slang suited to the South. Weather, trees, lakes, and mountains provide the background for down-home wisdom. Hunting, fishing, and farming terms get absorbed into Southern humor. Animals from the family dogs to farm chickens and hogs are fair game for one-liners. And while humor based on bodily functions is virtually universal, the Southern earthiness takes it to a new, no-holds-barred level. On balance, polite language has always resonated with the Southern culture.

The British influence on Southernism made writing this chapter an exercise in cultural clash for me. I grew up in Bermuda saying "down the road a piece." How could this be on a list of Southern sayings? I had flashbacks to childhood lectures when I read the familiar phrase, "Don't fly off the handle." My brother Joe and I were like "two peas in a pod," always in a hurry. We were told to "hold your horses," but that felt like being a 'bump on a log" to us. Too much in a rush to remember where we put our toys, my grandmother would sigh and say, "Can I hit you if I find them?" We knew she'd never lay a finger on us so we played the game and agreed. The lost item was usually in plain sight and she'd sigh again, "If it were a snake, it would've bit you." It was a wonderful Southern-style saying, but my grandmother never set foot in the South.

Why is there a similarity in sayings and slang between Bermuda and the South? The secret is in the phrases, words, names, and spelling of the British who colonized both places. Echoes of the English, Irish, and Scots remain today not only in isolated communities, but in many places where they settled, including New England and its Northern culture. The result is an unpredictable mix of idioms and sayings that almost defy categories and logic. For example, folks from Boston understand hardship as well as folks from Tennessee. However, only Southerners will use "folks" as the default term, but both will use the phrase, "been through the mill."

Given a Southern-ish grandfather, a Bostonian father, and a Bermudian mother, I didn't stand a chance. Sorting out the Southern, British, and Bermudian differences was impossible, especially since the English spoken in Bermuda when I was growing up was somewhere between the Victorian Jane Austen and the World War II Winston Churchill. I can't help but wonder why these Southernisms are familiar. Are they British, Bostonian, Bermudian, or Southern? Does it matter? Here is my rule of thumb for the New Southerner in a similar state of confusion: When Southerners claim an idiom is Southern, agree with them. Even if the saying has other origins, it's Southern enough.

Rather than search for the origins of these Southernisms, look at how they fit into Southern culture and why Southerners claim them as their own. They are better than a "passel" of museums "chock full" of cultural artifacts. Southernisms are a cultural anthropologist's dream come true. They come in a variety of styles from formal to crude. The formal style echoes its British origins. On the opposite end of the spectrum, the crude sayings often reflect the local culture with a side order of body humor. The two styles can coexist side-by-side, along with everything in between, ranging from colorful to outrageous. Their use is dictated by attitude and intent.

My family generally used the formal style. One of my grandmother's favorite finger-shaking sayings was, "Haste Makes Waste." The saying has a long history as an English proverb, teaching us that being too busy and too hasty can have dire consequences. My father's choice of an old English proverb was "Waste Not, Want Not". Either they were both very careful and quite slow or I tended towards the rash and frenzied. The years have shown me that it was the latter rather than the former. Since the formal style did not quite penetrate my young consciousness, I now collect a variety of haste-oriented sayings to remind me to take my time. Fortunately, here in the South, there is no lack of such idioms and all are memorable. Southern descriptions of being busy are sure to keep me grounded.

If you're this busy, stop now.

*Busy as a funeral home fan in July*

*Busier than a cat covering crap on a marble floor*

*Running around like a chicken with its head cut off*

And my favorite: *Busier than a one-legged man at a butt kickin' contest!*

The easy availability of "too busy" idioms doesn't mean that being too slow is necessarily tolerated. If I'm told that I'm "as slow as molasses," then I know to hurry up. This hasn't happened to me personally, as my love of speed and sense of urgency usually give real Southerners a headache. The sayings about hastiness have been applied to me far more frequently than those about being too slow. Many New Southerners will find themselves in the same leaky, speeding boat.

If you're the target of sayings like these, you've gone too far too fast:

*Don't bite off more than you can chew.*

*Don't count your chickens until they hatch.*

When you're given these warnings, it's time to back off and slow down. The discussion is definitely over and your insistence on making your point will be perceived as "Beating a dead horse." In my family, if the warnings to cease and desist were not headed, they would be followed by some in-your-face Yiddish expressions like "Enough already!" I got the message and "shut up," a phrase that is unacceptable in the South as "down-right" rude. Southerners aren't likely to say anything harsher than "hush" or "shhh." Not wanting to embarrass you by publicly acknowledging your foolishness, they may skip the verbal altogether and mime the message by putting their index finger to pursed lips.

Being rude should be avoided at all costs even when you're "so angry you could spit nails." Temper tantrums are often referred to as "fits" as if they were some kind of mental breakdowns. When you say that you had a "conniption fit" or "pitched a hissy fit," you were really, really angry. You were "madder than a wet hen." Regardless of your mental state or the excellent reasons for getting "all riled up," don't act on it, and don't be confrontational. If you're tempted to act out your anger, you're likely to be warned with another old British proverb turned Southernism, "Don't go off half-cocked." It refers to guns, not chickens. Take it very seriously and don't do something stupid.

I can still hear Gramp all these decades later asking, "What the Sam Hill do you think you're doing?" I never questioned who or what Sam Hill was, nor did I answer the question. The point was to stop whatever you were doing because it was beyond stupid, beyond any explanation that would save you. There were any number of variations of the question, "What in God's name are you doing?" and the Britishly understated, "What, pray tell, are you doing?" This last version was delivered in a hushed, slow, deliberate tone of voice intended to make your blood run cold at being "found out." A true Southerner has no need to raise their voice to put a stop to foolishness. Do not be lulled into complacency by the soft voice and polite tone. You've been caught like a rat in a trap, with less chance for escape than the rat.

Descriptions of stupid abound with an almost infinite number of variations, each more exaggerated and fantastical than the last. Why be "dumber than a rock" when you can be "dumber than a box of rocks"? Why settle for "clueless" when you can say you "don't know to come in out of the rain"? Don't stop at being plain clumsy when you can be "like a bull in a china shop."

And don't be surprised if all of the above are used at the same time, plus a few more. It's a perpetual competition for the most creative put-downs, the most entertaining insult. My favorite is "He's so dumb, he could throw himself on the ground and miss."

I hope no one says that about me, but I'll never know because insults like these are said "behind your back," not "to your face." At first blush, it would seem that the Southern aversion to being rude would dictate adherence to the universal adage "If you can't say something nice, don't say anything at all." However, the temptation is far too great to resist and there is a built-in mechanism for saying virtually anything about anyone. All you have to do is say "bless their heart" and you have given notice that the insults to follow will be memorable and probably not repeatable. They're certainly not to be repeated to the person in question.

The only repeatable insults are those you tell about yourself. Self-deprecatory humor goes over well in the South as harmless fun and a valuable distraction from one's failings. When one of my employees warned the office that he's tone deaf and "can't carry a tune in a bucket," he was just getting warmed up. He then proceeded to serenade me with the worst rendition of "Happy Birthday" I'd ever heard. A wide grin took up his whole face when I sat motionless and speechless. Finally, I folded my arms on the table, laid my head down on them, and laughed until I cried. My body language was much appreciated. Settling for a polite giggle under the circumstances wouldn't have done justice to the gross understatement.

Sometimes the Southernisms go way beyond rude. The polite, friendly culture of the South has some of the most earthy, crude stories, jokes, and zingers that I've heard anywhere. The humor based on bodily functions is particularly outrageous. For better or worse, my British-Bermuda brain comes to a screeching halt at the body humor. Yes, they're often hysterically funny, but I would never, ever say them out loud. No Southern lady, young girl, or educated person of any age would repeat these sayings. However, if prompted, most of them could come up with a few highly entertaining and very wicked phrases. You could have "knocked me over with a feather" when my financial advisor, a true Southern lady with multiple degrees, offered her favorite Southernism, "He has his head so far up his a**, that when he opens his mouth, you can see his face."

What does it mean for New Southerners when they come to a culture where there are so many ways to describe stupid? Where etiquette can be suspended in favor of cutting humor? It means that an understanding of duality is required. The South is the most polite region in the United States. Southerners prefer a style that is soft-spoken, a bit vague, and modestly unassuming. However, the stereotype of being and/or sounding stupid is unfounded. There is an edgy, cutting edge side to the South that you may or not see. Trust that it is there and plan accordingly. Take the soft-spoken at face value whenever possible, but be alert for signs that there is more to the situation than meets the eye.

Check out the Southern-style comedians who make a lot of money adapting Southernisms for commercial use. Jeff Foxworthy is famous for with his jokes about "You Know You're a Redneck if ..." Ron White and his "Can't Fix Stupid" routines are on television regularly. Both tour the country frequently to perform for audiences who may or not have ever set foot in the South. Southernisms attract fans from all over the country and from metropolitan areas that have no connection to the land that gave birth to these sayings. Southernisms are being bought and sold widely, even though they are culturally specific.

## Chapter 14: *The Performance: Why It's Always Time for Your Close-Up*

Performance of social rituals and adherence to traditions may seem antithetical to the friendliness of the South; the apparent informality and emphasis on relationships. However, as in many cultures that have experienced periods of relative isolation, patterns of behavior are woven into the existing social fabric. The friendliness is part of the fabric, but it should not be mistaken for the fabric itself. Rather, friendliness is simply the most visible part of a vast network of rituals, customs, and traditions that make up Southern culture. As esoteric as this bit of cultural anthropology wisdom sounds, living in this environment illustrates its personal impact on a daily basis. Allow me to demonstrate with a few stories.

I park the car at the convention center for the latest in a series of awards banquets and check the mirror for a last minute inspection. Did my hair get messed up on the drive over? A silly question because my curly silver hair is more eccentric than stylish, but my veneer of Southern-lady kicks in regardless. I check that there is no food stuck in my teeth. It's not very likely, but ever since my lunch with real Southern ladies who passed around a mirror to check their teeth mutually after the meal, I'm more vigilant. The visual, the first impression, is a key component of body language everywhere. But the South takes the visuals—your physical presentation—to new heights.

Remembering last year's fiasco, I make sure no tags are sticking out of the collar or sleeves of my new suit. I was taken aside with stern words by one of the organizers. I'm grateful it was done more or less in private, and before too many people could see me. The better known you are, the more scrutiny you receive, and even if you don't hear the comments, assume they're being made. With that in mind, I check to see that my earrings are properly in place, the matching necklace is centered, and that my watch and bracelet are not riding up on either arm. For Southern women, jewelry is second nature. They do not, as I often do, get so distracted writing that they throw on clothes at the last minute and arrive with empty pierced ear lobes and wrists devoid of all embellishment, not even a watch.

I have not always paid close attention, and I suppose anyone in town can attest to that fact. The last time I went to get my hair done, a euphemism for a twice-annual quick haircut, the beautician sat me down for a heart-to-heart talk. "We all know you're smart," he said. "Don't you want to be beautiful, too?" At my blank stare, he informed me that Southern women plan their wardrobes like a military maneuver. Their battle campaigns include estimates of public appearances, formal affairs, business meetings, and informal gatherings. When I responded by saying I could care less, I was informed that I would not be allowed to prepare for an upcoming formal ceremony without adult supervision. What followed was a wildly educational trip to the mall and a very successful event, judging from the surprised and pleased looks on the faces around me. As the proud owner of a dress that was worn once and has hung in my closet for fifteen years, I can safely say that you can learn as much from my miscues as from an entire library of business etiquette books.

Do you like to experiment with new looks and accessories? What about perfumes, colognes, or aftershaves? Unless you're a teenager, aim for cautious, subtle, and understated. Otherwise, the reaction can be unexpectedly blunt in a region known for its grace and politeness. The last time I tried a flower-scented hair spray, it was magnified by my body chemistry, and I impressed an entire elevator full of people. One gentleman couldn't take it any longer and asked loudly, "Who's that smell?" The bodies parted until I stood alone in the middle of the elevator. He came up to me and sniffed my hair. "Very nice!" When I smiled and thanked him, this perfect stranger, reached out to test my curls. "Are these real?"

Personal curiosity is virtually unlimited here and when combined with the never-met-a-stranger worldview, the result is memorable. It can be invasive and highly entertaining, depending on your perspective and mood that day. Regardless of the time or place, there is no point in avoiding the culture's visual imperatives; resistance is futile. Plan accordingly and try to see the humor in such situations since getting huffy will only make matters worse.

As cultural miscues are impossible to avoid completely, it's wise to practice a variety of responses that rely on the ever-popular self-deprecating humor. When I showed up one Saturday morning at Sabbath services wearing leggings, a short skirt, and form-fitting sweater, the response was, "What the Hell happened to you? You look like an escapee from a college dorm." Now my fashion consultant, my daughter, had assured me that the outfit was mighty fine, but she lives up North in New England Massachusetts. Recognizing a culture clash moment, I responded with a sheepish grin, not just a smile. Then I told my friend, who still thinks of me as executive director of the Jewish Federation, "Yeah, I'm doing my writer thing. I have to dress like this to qualify for the artist of the week award."

Facial expressions are a lively part of the language in the South. This may pose a challenge for those who are used to an unexpressive norm. At rest, the Southern face is what my grandmother used to call "pleasant." Even strangers have a slight smile and their gaze will meet yours before moving on. When a stranger interacts with you, the smile will become wider, the gaze last longer, and the eyebrows may rise very slightly to indicate interest in what you're saying. If they recognize you, the smile will widen to show teeth, the eyes will crinkle with the smile, and a full greeting may follow.

Greetings can be complicated in the South. There is no standard set of words and gestures that can be used for all occasions. The choices made for the greeting are based on relationships. My greetings tend to be more formal than most of my colleagues' and friends' are. Whether it's a reflection of my upbringing as a British colonial, my many years in New York, or my natural reserve as an introvert, the result is the same. I am often corrected, or upon seeing the confusion on people's faces, self-corrected.

In a business context where I do not know my associates well, I extend my hand for a handshake. This is one of the more universally understood greetings and it would seem difficult to go wrong with the handshake. However, relationships form quite quickly in the South and the formality of the handshake becomes a culture clash moment. I have been told to "Put that away!" when I extended my hand and found myself engulfed in a huge hug. I have had people from politicians to artists accept my hand, but look positively forlorn until I added a hug.

As I amble into the convention center, I take my time, unbutton my stylish purple trench coat, and prepare for a major greeting festival. After all, this is a women's event and relationships are virtually assumed. I'm given my table assignment, but I don't bother sitting down.

We're all wandering about, greeting each other. Hugs abound.

I hug a city councilwoman and flashbulbs go off. I am apparently mistaken for the well-known "Purple Lady" who also has silver hair and has branded herself over the years by wearing only purple. When the mistaken identity is realized, there's just a shrug of the shoulders and a comment. "We thought you were other Purple Lady." More photos are taken. Apparently, I'm close enough to the real thing so that it's all good. I just smile more broadly, knowing that I will mistake identities more than once in the next hour, but it will turn out fine.

An eager and sincere woman rushes up to me, explaining how sorry she was that she couldn't assist me in my upcoming project. Did I get her e-mail explaining why? "I totally understand," I respond. "Thank you so much for the e-mail. I appreciate the time you took to consider my request." In reality, I have no idea who this person is, what project I discussed with her, or what I requested. Maybe I received her e-mail, maybe not. Yet, understand that my inability to remember was irrelevant to the situation. The key to success was to say the right things to preserve the relationship in good Southern fashion.

I can recall a time when I was too timid to plunge intrepidly into the room, all the way to the seats of power at the head table. I extend my hand continually, watching the facial expressions for the correctly calibrated response. To the "pleasant" faces, I say what a pleasure it is to meet and give my name. To those with a bigger smile, but remain a mystery to me, I say what a pleasure it is to see them, and it's been far too long since we've talked. If they don't move along, I add that we really should get together for lunch, to which we both happily agree and part ways with matching smiles. Newcomers tend to take "Let's get together" at face value and feel slighted when nothing happens. Understand that you have not failed and the person has not lied. This is a social-fabric ritual; develop the relationship to make the ritual come to life.

What does social performance look like in the work place? You do not see the handshakes or the hugging among colleagues who work together regularly. There may be, however, a great deal of conversation. People catch up on weekend sports, share notes on the latest movie, and compare notes on holiday plans. They may talk about their kids, spouses, parents, cousins, or other family members, careening between pride and despair over their antics or health. As permitted, their desk, cubby, and/or office will be decorated with family photos and memorabilia. The bottom line, small talk is woven into the fabric of the workplace. You may wonder why you have to listen to all of these personal stories, sometimes repeated many times over. Keep in mind that you were chosen to participate in a social ritual at the heart of Southern culture, so be respectful even as you nudge folks towards vital deadlines. For my Southern readers, let your natural enthusiasm be expressed in your tone of voice rather than a flood of details.

Tone of voice is no small matter in the South, nor is enthusiasm. Showing discouragement, depression, and disgust in your voice should be reserved for people you know very well, and even then, in moderation. A monotone response to "Hi! How are you?" can be perceived as unfriendly with an intensity ranging from casual disinterest to outright hostility. Responding that you're "okay" can also distance you from your colleagues, who may assume the opposite—that you are not okay. Even responding that you're "good" should be accompanied by a smile and an upward lilt to your voice. Telling people that you're "great" or "wonderful" may seem over-the-top back home, but the exaggerations work well here.

Newcomers to the South who are used to a faster pace may feel impatience, frustration, and anger. Can you raise your voice? Adopt a snarky or sarcastic tone? Use the shaming voice you save for badly behaved kids and pets? The answer is ideally, none of the above, especially in public. Embarrassing people is always a risky move, but in the South, it could be your last move. Friendliness is integral to social interaction here, but real trust must be earned. Trust is easily lost in a society where saving face is a major tool for coexistence. Apologies are usually accepted gracefully, but wariness may take years to dissipate.

Performance Strategies

1. When you've had enough small talk at the office, find a way to stop the flow of chatter that preserves dignity. Popular phrases include:
    a. "I'm late for my next meeting, but remind me about this later."
    b. "Let's talk more when I don't have this deadline."
    c. "I have a phone call that I'll have to take in a couple of minutes." I know one executive who actually programs her phone to ring at ten-minute intervals, just to make sure she has a face-saving escape.
2. When you don't want to attend a function or accept an invitation, find a way to refuse that preserves dignity. Popular phrases include:
    a. "We're having out-of-town guests that weekend."
    b. "We're going out of town."
    c. "I'm already scheduled to be somewhere."
    d. "I have to work that day."

## Chapter 15: *The Relationship: How Are You Fixin' to Fix It?*

Southern culture is built on The Relationship; messy, complex, convoluted, long-standing relationships. If you don't understand why you had a dozen RSVPs and only two people showed up, re-examine the relationships involved. If your analysis of missed deadlines doesn't make sense, re-visit your relationships with colleagues and employees. If your e-mails aren't answered, pick up the phone and talk one human being to another. Better yet, meet over coffee and expand that relationship; make it work and fix it if needed. Does this sound time consuming to you? It should, because it is.

How should New Southerners understand time in the South? There is a must-hear country song with the title of an old saying "timing is everything." In Southern style, the song is about relationships and God, timing and luck. It's about fate, faith, and love. It's not about having time, making time, or keeping time. The song expresses the relationship-based values of Southern culture as applied to time. It should not come as a surprise that many New Southerners will encounter a culture clash over time management.

One long-time Southerner pointed out that time management may mean more efficiency for a few, but means more work for most others. Clearing off your desk is merely an invitation for more projects to end up on it. An endless stream of assignments is a hazard in the South where the priority is on the quality of life rather than a nose-to-the-grindstone approach to work. Overlapping deadlines with no end in sight are not only depressing, but they relegate the Southern priority of work-life balance to the bottom of the to-do list.

Multi-tasking in the South is quite distinctive, given the emphasis on family values. Workers will often take on a part-time job in addition to the regular employment, and second full-time job shouldn't come as a surprise. It's common to both work and go to school full-time. Many are entrepreneurial and will have their own business in addition to their job. The commercial enterprise can be anything and everything including tending the family farm, making jewelry, performing in a band, and caring for children while parents work. The goal is to support loved ones in as many ways imaginable and still maintain precious family time.

The resulting sense of timing ranges from a laid-back stroll to a Type-A mad dash. How do New Southerners navigate the challenges of relationships and timing? There are three key elements necessary for a successful strategy: 1) The Intent 2) the Fix, and 3) The Context. Each element has vital cues for effective long-term interaction.

*Language*

1. Look for the Intent

Language in the South about time has a colorful vagueness. I haven't experienced the classic Southernism, "fixin' to" anywhere else. The saying describes a state of mind that is thinking about getting around to thinking about doing something, somehow. While "fixin' to" isn't used by everyone in the South, New Southerners find that the mindset is quite common, even in the workplace. It's helpful to think of "fixing' to" as the equivalent to getting driving directions that feature the phrase "over yonder." The phrases are intended to acknowledge your concerns and questions, but it has little to do with actually planning for them.

Relationships here focus more on the intent than the outcome. Yes, it's wonderful if you actually finish a task on time, arrive on time, call at the expected hour, and don't change appointments at the last minute. But failing to do so doesn't necessarily bury an ongoing relationship. If the perception remains that you intended to call, be on time, and finish the project, there is still hope. How is this perception created and maintained? Observe how it's done and learn from what is truly an art form of Southern communication.

2. Use The Fix

If you've missed your timing there are four possible strategies you can use to fix the mistake and maintain the relationship: 1) The Apology 2) The Excuse 3) The Humor, and 4) The Compliment

*The Apology*

An apology is absolutely required and should always be accepted, at least on a superficial level. I recommend that "I'm sorry" be embellished and inflated to "I'm so sorry" or "I'm so very sorry." You can switch to a more formal phrasing by saying in a serious tone "I owe you an apology." Finally, you can add gestures that help convey your apologies, place your hand on their arm lightly, press your hand to your heart, or cup your check with your hand to express disbelief that you had missed the mark. All of this is preliminary to the Excuse.

*The Excuse*

The excuses or explanations will range from the simple "I totally lost track of time" to the dramatic "I had to go my grandmother's funeral." I know people who have gone to their grandmother's funeral a half dozen times, but the excuse is still a good one. Sharing personal information about family may be done freely, startling those not used to it. Relatives get preferential treatment in the hierarchy of relationships. Deference is given to helping family members who require medical treatment whether it's a doctor's appointment, a hospital stay, an emergency room visit, a funeral visitation, or taking care of the children of a relative in any of these circumstances. If you are on the receiving end of one of these excuses, listen attentively and let your face express your interest and sympathy. No words are needed in this family-oriented culture.

The amount of detail in the explanation depends on the depth of the relationship you have together. That depth dictates the Context of your relationship. When you know someone well, the relationship is informal. That means hugs instead of handshakes and a greeting of "Hey" rather than a reserved "Good morning, sir." Among True Southerners, strangers are relatively rare, so it's quite accurate and common to describe people with the phrase "He never met a stranger."

A formal excuse is short with little explanation and it is my default mode. Last week, I showed up at the last minute to an open house showing off the newly refurbished Engel Stadium, which appears in the movie 42. Friends had participated in the planning and I wanted to show my support by attending. I told them how sorry I was to come so late in the afternoon, but I had misplaced my glasses. There was silence; they waited for it to sink in that we were better friends than I had realized. Once I understood, I proceeded to tell a story about what happened to the glasses, where I had put them, why anyone with half a brain would have remembered, but I was obviously too pitiful to perform at that level and I was fortunate to have made it to this wonderful event before the doors closed and everyone had gone home. I was then given a tour and I made sure to marvel at the sights with very audible *ooohs* and *aaahs*.

### The Humor

Long-time friends may resort to humor when the timing goes wrong. The jokes will often be self-deprecatory, harmless extensions of the apology and excuses. "You know I can't find my way out of a paper bag. Did you really think I'd be on time?" A friend might respond, "How come you were so early? We had bets going on how late you'd be. If you'd been ten minutes later, I'd have won."

Count yourself lucky if you have a long-running relationship with a True Southerner who knows you well enough to move on to the Practical Joke. So here's a toast to Stuart Bush, chair of my Planning Committee for Chattanooga's Jewish Cultural Center: *I did warn you when you made off with my grocery cart in Whole Foods with that butter-would-melt-my-mouth look that I was going to put you in this book. And, Stuart, you owe me because I'm not mentioning the time ... well, enough said. You know I appreciate you.*

Compliments range from the general "You look great" to the specific "Your presentation was the best I've heard all day." Each compliment should be received by a "thank you" regardless of how exaggerated, outrageous, or unlikely they may seem. To ensure continued social interaction, return the compliment. Feel free to embellish, admire, and prolong the conversation. Apply your smile liberally in the process.

3. Assess The Context

Cultural anthropology defines a high-context culture as one that has many unspoken cues and an indirect communication style. Look at the South as a poster child for the high-context culture. In this context, intent counts almost as much as commitment. Yes, it's wonderful for you to attend when you have sent an RSVP that you will be there. But, the RSVP is more an intention than an announcement. Unless the event is an intimate dinner party at a person's home, where the knowing the numbers are crucial, it's helpful to assume that the RSVP is be limited to a friendly show of interest. I was amused when a friend and colleague, Ron Harris of Blue Cross BlueShield of Tennessee, introduced as, "Here is Deborah Levine. If she says she's coming, she'll actually be there." Apparently, marrying intent and commitment with the RSVP is a worthy tag line in the South.

How do Southerners know what to expect in such a high-context culture? When you've grown up around the clues, you don't really have to think about their meaning. They are part of the regional language; they're loud and clear. If there's doubt, the Southerner can use their intuition, which is a fancy name for unconscious knowledge. The gestalt, the universe of clues, is present in each individual in the high-context culture, and is an excellent source of emotional intelligence. It's no accident that the phrase "Gut Check" originated in the South, with the famous football coach of the University of Alabama, Bear Bryant. When in doubt, go with your gut. If it's not perfect, the result will be "close enough." The preference for intuition, for approximation, works well in an insular, high-context community where the variables are finite and well known.

What happens if you're not from around here and can't use intuitive reasoning or do a "gut check" on your decisions? What if you are like me, brought into the region to build a business, plant, or infrastructure that must have a successful interface with the community? I wondered if my minimal understanding of the Context would be a hindrance in leading the project. As the Federation Executive Director planning of a cultural center, I sought as much community input as possible through sub-committees and forums. But, I also found that some of the skills and decision-making required favored an outsider, a transplant who may or may not stay permanently. If you are a transplant or expat hired for this role, you will be given flexibility to do what is needed, but respect for Southern culture is still required.

The plan was a complex one, laying out both short-term and long-term goals, designing benchmarks, and deadlines as well as negotiating land use, building design, and security features. The project required an anticipation of the use, accessibility, and impact on the community. A timeline was needed that would provide for sustainability over decades. An emphasis on the future was vital for the project, but predictions of demographic trends and economic growth were not common topics of conversation at that time. My situation required developing an extensive planning model that has become more familiar to the community.

Many New Southerners feel at a disadvantage coming into the region without friends and relatives to support them. They know that developing relationships should be a major priority and they're anxious about the process. However, a certain amount of distance and space to make controversial decisions and set up new expectations of timing and action can be liberating to all parties during the intense planning period. Today, planning skills are more prevalent and expectations have been shaped by the large number of national and international industries locating in the South. Time has changed the environment and will continue to do so. However, the underlying cultural values remain. It's wise to be wary of going too fast and getting too far ahead of the community.

## 8 TIMING TIPS FOR NEW SOUTHERNERS

1. Designate multiple deadlines so that you can discover problems along the way to the ultimate deadline.
2. Anticipate that Southerners will be eager to please, slow to share their failures and mortified at public censure.
3. Add efficiency to meetings by consistently starting on time. Accept apologies for tardiness with a smile, but don't start over. Budget time for after the meeting to talk to individuals if needed.
4. Keep your sense of humor with jokes about your newness. Consider them a sign of affection.
5. Understand that silence after several attempts is your answer; it's not just an oversight.
6. Give compliments liberally as positive reinforcement, especially when there are deadlines that are important to you and your company.
7. Accept that many of your efforts will take more time than you originally anticipated. Plan accordingly.
8. Don't assume that a lack of comment when you miscalculate and/or make a mistake means that nobody noticed. Rather, assume that everyone noticed and is too polite to draw attention to it. Don't ignore your mistake. Fix problems in private one-on-one conversations. Public discussion of mistakes can be counterproductive on all sides unless they are minor technicalities.

# Chapter 16: *The Secret Ingredient: Why Storytelling is the Key*

As a college freshman, I dreamed for years of being a famous cultural anthropologists like Margaret Mead; her work was more fascinating than any adventure movie. I asked to join a research class in an isolated area of India, but the professor just laughed. She had no intention of "inserting" an untrained freshman into a field study where she might make a mess. Illness derailed me from joining a new research project in the Chiapas Highlands of Mexico that was created by the Folklore & Mythology Department the following year. I wanted to see for myself how reading, hearing, and recording stories of a culture meant capturing its essence. My time in the South has made up for that disappointment many times over. Stories are everywhere here, and they hold the essence of the culture not just for folklorists, but for every New Southerner and anyone remotely curious about the South.

Whether in literature, speeches, tales, or songs, the stories of the South are vivid blossoms on vines rooted deep into the complex social fabric. Want to understand Southern culture? Listen, read, and then listen some more. Southern literature has woven together the themes of history and an agrarian society of race, gender, and family since the beginning of the colonization of the region. When I asked a Southern friend to give me a list of the must-reads of famous novelists in relatively recent history, here is what she shared with me and I pass on to you.

1. The Sound and the Fury - William Faulkner (1929)
2. Gone with the Wind - Margaret Mitchell (1936)
3. Native Son – Richard Wright (1940)
4. The Member of the Wedding – Carson McCullers (1946)
5. Invisible Man – Ralph Ellison (circa 1952)
6. To Kill a Mockingbird - Harper Lee (1960)
7. The Optimist's Daughter - Eudora Welty (1973)
8. Roots - Alex Haley (1976)
9. The Color Purple - Alice Walker (1982 )
10. Fair and Tender Ladies – Lee Smith (1988)

It's not unusual to find Southerners who can rattle off lists of famous writers from the South. It's not unusual to find that your Southern acquaintances have writing aspirations. There are book clubs, poetry groups, public readings, open mikes, and storytelling events easily accessible almost anywhere in the region. They're scattered around neighborhood centers, in churches, and nonprofits. Supported by arts organizations, patrons, universities, and municipal agencies, the groups periodically blossom into festivals, conferences, and competitions.

The poetry reading I attended a few Saturdays ago was at the back of a café in the downtown of a mini-village section of an historic district. As we sipped our coffee, we listened to the mountain music of a homegrown band and the work of homegrown poets. Music and literature are frequent partners in the South. The lyrics, prose, speeches, and poetry have a musicality that blend well together.

Some argue that the changes in the South, the many New Southerners, the international connections, and global economy mean that there is no longer a Southern voice. Anthropology does teach us that inserting externals into an isolated society puts into motion changes that are powerful and extensive. Yes, many famous contemporary Southern writers don't write about the South: Thomas Wolfe, Truman Capote, Ann Rice, and John Grisham. But it can also be argued that it's the telling, not just the Southern themes, that distinguish the Southern writer. The compelling themes, absorbing characters, quotable prose, and memorable plots that are part of the region's long legacy of storytelling have become a major export to national and international fans.

When you listen to even the simplest, informal story of the Southerner, you are hearing that legacy. If you embrace storytelling not only by listening, but by learning, practicing, and using stories, you will start to speak the language of the South.

What is it like to learn the art of storytelling? Years ago, the urge to make it personal became too much to resist and I asked permission to tell a story at a local cultural festival. The organizer of the storytellers, Vincent Ivan Phipps, came to my home to videotape me so that I could see what I looked like, but I believe that was a polite cover for whether he would give his approval for my joining the performers. I passed the test and I will always grateful to Vincent for setting me on the storytelling road. Many of the Southerners involved in the festival drew their content from family stories and history. I did the same. They practiced not only their content, but the timing, the tone of voice, the gestures, and audience interaction. Some had props and others interspersed their performances with music. A few read from books they had published. They performed as if they were rocking on their porches on a summer evening, sharing their stories with friends and neighbors. I'm pretty sure they actually did practice on their porches; I eventually did, too.

I learned to appreciate how every detail gives shape to the story. I learned how storytellers' beliefs and values are embedded in family stories, historical tales, and landscape descriptions. Their characters are drawn with empathy, humor, and a wide range of colorful metaphors designed to tug at the audience. I learned to enjoy engaging the audience and to take the time to really see them, approach them, and involve them in the storytelling process. And I became aware that stories permeate every nook and cranny in the South; every home, workplace, and social gathering.

Storytelling became a basic building block for my workshops on cross-cultural communication in the South. Stories became the delivery mode for lessons on going global, and now, for *Going Southern*. I teach storytelling as knowledge management across cultural boundaries. My storytelling techniques provide tools for conflict management and wise decision making. Above all, I use the stories to acculturate New Southerners and help those who work with them. They listen, learn, and try telling a few themselves. *Going Southern* just isn't right without the stories. Storytelling is at the core of my No-Mess training and I couldn't unleash your inner cultural anthropologist without it.

# ACKNOWLEDGEMENTS

I would like to express my thanks to several writers for their support in the making of *Going Southern,* including poets Wendell Brown and Darius Myrick, German journalist Beate Ziehres, Southern author Deb Hunter, and storytelling guru Vincent Ivan Phipps.

I am honored to have had the opportunity to work with the board and staff of the Jewish Federation of Greater Chattanooga as its Executive Director. Thank you to the Federation's planning committee of the Jewish Cultural Center and its Chair, Stuart Bush, and for the ongoing co-sponsorship of my Global Leadership/Cross Cultural workshops in the Center. My appreciation also to the Institute of Southern Jewish Life and the Director of its History Department, Dr. Stuart Rockoff, for research assistance & guidance.

Many thanks to the City of East Ridge for the opportunity to serve on its History Center planning committee, for syndication of my American Diversity Report by ERMA (East Ridge Merchants Association), and for my rewarding years as the East Ridge community correspondent to The Chattanooga Times Free Press.

Many thanks for interviews that supported the book: Alnoor Dhanani, president of Double Cola; Dianne

Irvine, Former Senior Attorney of Harvard University, Eleanor McCallie Cooper, Former President of Sister Cities/Chattanooga, Rev. Paul McDaniel, Pastor of Second Missionary Baptist Church, and Ruth Holmberg of Chattanooga, Former Editor-in-Chief of *The Chattanooga Times*.

The beta test of *Going Southern* training provided invaluable research for the book and was made possible by Terry Olsen, Attorney of Olsen Law Firm and incoming Chair of Immigration Section/TN Bar Association. Thanks also to the Urban League/Chattanooga for partnering with the youth version of cross-cultural training. I greatly appreciate the specialists who co-taught with me during the development phase, including Thinking Media's president, Sheila Boyington, and experts associated with Volkswagen Chattanooga: Coco Chen from China and, especially, Andrea Jagla from Germany.

I am also grateful to the intercultural consulting companies, Global LT and dfa/Dean Foster Associates for the privilege of representing them in Tennessee to train our growing number of international executives.

Thanks also to my editor, Beth Lynne, EdD, of bzhercules.com, and my cover artist, Alex Loza of Hoopla PR.

# ABOUT THE AUTHOR

DEBORAH J. LEVINE is an award-winning author and editor of the *American Diversity Report*. Her articles on cultural diversity are published in academic journals, popular magazines, and newspapers in the U.S. and internationally. Brought up in the British colony of Bermuda, she obtained advanced degrees in anthropology, urban planning, and religion in the United States. Deborah served as an executive in Jewish agencies in several regions and is currently headquartered in Tennessee where she trains international executives coming into the South and aspiring global leaders going global. Deborah designs creative resources such as the *Matrix Model Management System: Guide to Cross Cultural Wisdom, Inspire your Inner Global Leader,* and the series, *Going Southern: the No-Mess Guide to Success in the South.* A passionate innovator, Deborah created the Southeast Women's Council on Diversity, The DuPage/Chicago Interfaith Resource Network, the Chattanooga Global Leadership Class, the Youth Multicultural Video Contest, and the Cross Cultural School of the South. She is the recipient of awards from the Tennessee Economic Council on Women, Girls Inc./Chattanooga, American Planning Association/Chicago, and the National Catholic Press Association. Deborah serves on the Diversity Task Force of Volkswagen Chattanooga, and was chosen as a 2013 Champion of Diversity by diversitybusiness.com.

## Index

acculturation, 9, 16, 136
African American Vernacular English, 79
Alabama, 28, 30, 32, 36, 49, 52, 72, 76, 105, 109, 110, 111, 125, 182
American Diversity Report, 70, 79, 131, 136, 190, 192
*American Experience*, 57
Antebellum Era, 51
Appalachian, 4, 52, 53, 94, 95, 117
Arkansas, 28, 30
Armstrong, Louis, 121
Atlanta, 55, 56, 59, 60, 75, 77, 88, 105, 109, 111, 121, 135
Attucks, Crispus, 51
Augusta National Golf Club, 126
Bacon, Nathaniel, 52
Berea College, 95
Berke, Andy, 104
Berkley, Sir Maurice, 48
Bermuda, 13, 14, 15, 20, 24, 27, 46, 47, 104, 105, 152, 158, 159, 164, 192
Berry, Chuck, 122
Big Picture, 97, 128, 131, 134,
135, 138, 139, 140
Black churches, 108
Black-Jewish Coalition, 106, 107
Bluegrass, 117
Blues, 117
British influence, 158
Brooks, Garth, 118
*Brown vs. the Board of Education*, 107
Brown, James, 122
Brown, John, 51
Brown, Wendell A., 82
Bryant, Bear, 182
Cajun, 96
Capote, Truman, 187
Carpetbaggers, 57
Carter Family, 117
Cash, Johnny, 117
Cash, June Carter, 117
Charles, Ray, 121
Chattanooga, 3, 11, 12, 15, 20, 21, 25, 28, 29, 40, 41, 55, 56, 61, 62, 63, 70, 89, 91, 104, 106, 112, 122, 130, 132, 137, 147, 180, 190, 191, 192
Cherokee, 36, 37, 38, 39, 41, 134
Chickamauga National Military Park, 29

Christian, 76, 77, 90, 91, 99, 100, 101, 103, 108, 112, 113
Civil Rights Movement, 7, 69, 75, 106
Civil War, 7, 25, 26, 28, 29, 30, 33, 48, 51, 53, 55, 56, 57, 59, 71, 74, 89, 104, 108
Clark, Roy, 117
Clooney, George, 119
Coltrane, John, 121
Confederate, 30, 31, 33, 55, 66
CORE, 76
country music, 116, 117, 118
Cross Cultural School of the South, 136, 192
cultural anthropology, 7, 166
Dean, Vince, 91
Deep South, 32, 33, 34, 49, 95
Dhanani, Alnoor, 129
Dixie, 27, 28, 32
Dixie Land, 27, 32
*Driving Miss Daisy*, 86
East Ridge, 20, 62, 63, 89, 90, 91, 92, 112, 124, 135, 190
Ellison, Ralph, 186
Empire Day, 14, 24
Expat, 8, 131, 134

Expats, 128, 131, 139
Faulkner, William, 186
Fitzgerald, Ella, 121
fixin' to, 177
Florida, 30, 32, 33, 104, 121
Fort Sumter, 30, 31, 32
Foster, Stephen, 120
Franke, Leo, 104
Franklin, Aretha, 121
Georgia, 13, 28, 29, 30, 32, 37, 38, 39, 43, 49, 52, 55, 60, 67, 88, 110, 111, 124, 125, 126, 129
Glass Jr., Bill, 41
Going Southern, 3, 4, 7, 8, 9, 10, 11, 22, 23, 68, 85, 189, 190, 191, 192
golf, 39, 123, 124, 125
*Gone with the Wind*, 49, 57, 186
Gospel, 117, 121
Graceland, 116
Grady, Henry, 58
Gramp, 20, 24, 162
Great Smoky Mountains National Park, 53
Grisham, John, 187
Gut Check, 182
Haley, Alex, 186
Hill, Faith, 118
hillbillies, 52

Holmberg, Ruth, 106
Hunter, Deb, 134, 135
Institute of Southern Jewish Life, 104, 190
Internationals, 37, 69, 85, 99, 108, 110, 131, 136, 137, 146
Jack Daniels Whiskey, 125
Jackson, Mahalia, 121
Jamestown, 46, 47, 48, 52, 53
Jewish Federation of Greater Chattanooga, 107, 169, 190
Jim Crow, 73, 74
Kentucky, 30, 94, 109, 110, 119, 120, 125
King, Rev. Dr. Martin Luther, 70
Knight, Gladys, 121
Ku Klux Klan, 73
Lee, Harper, 186
Levine, Deborah, 181
Little Richard, 122
Louisiana, 30, 32, 49, 50, 73, 95, 103, 110, 111, 129
Lynn, Loretta, 117
Malloy, Myer Gramp, 19
Martin Luther King Day, 77
Mason Dixon Line, 26

Mason-Dixon Line, 25, 27
McCreery, Scott, 118
McCullers, Carson, 186
Mead, Margaret, 185
Memphis, 13, 28, 61, 75, 105, 121
Missionary Ridge, 28, 29, 30, 89
Mississippi, 13, 28, 30, 32, 49, 52, 65, 76, 109, 110, 111, 122
Missouri, 30, 102, 122
Mitchell, Margaret, 186
Mizpah Congregation, 106, 112
Muddy Waters, 122
Museum of Railroads, 55
My Old Kentucky Home, 120
Myrick, Darius, 83
NAACP, 75, 78, 107
NASCAR, 125
Nash, Diane, 70
Native American, 34, 36, 37, 39, 41, 42, 43, 44, 50, 65
Naturalized Southerners, 128, 129, 139
New Echota, 38, 39
New Orleans, 13, 50, 60, 75, 96, 109, 121, 146
New Southerner, 8, 33, 66, 68, 99,

100, 101, 107, 118, 149, 157, 159, 185
New Southerners, 7, 9, 23, 24, 36, 39, 41, 55, 61, 62, 64, 87, 98, 108, 114, 115, 125, 128, 136, 138, 149, 151, 161, 164, 175, 176, 177, 183, 184, 187, 189
Non-Southerner, 36
North Carolina, 30, 53, 111, 121, 129
*O Brother, Where art Thou?*, 119
Obama, Barack, 72
Oklahoma, 36, 37, 38, 41
Oklahoma Historical Society, 38
*Old South*, 45, 49, 51, 53, 54, 119
PBS, 51, 57, 72, 73, *See* American Experience
Phipps, Vincent Ivan, 188
plantations, 25, 49, 50, 57, 74
Plantations Destrehan, Drayton Hall, L'Hermitage, Magnolia, The Hermitage, 50
Plymouth, 45, 46
Pocahontas, 46, 47
Presley, Elvis, 116
railroads, 59, 65, 74
Rascal Flatts, 123

Returning Southerner, 135
Returning Southerners, 8, 128, 134, 140
Rhythm & Blues, 117, 121
Rice, Ann, 187
Ring of Fire, 117
Rockabilly, 117
Rockoff, Stuart R., 104
Rolfe, John, 47
Rolling Stones, 122
Scruggs, Earl, 118
segregation, 25, 73, 106
Skaggs, Ricky, 118
Smith, Captain John, 46
Smith, Lee, 186
SNCC, (Student Nonviolent Coordination Committee), 76
South Carolina, 30, 31, 32, 49, 50, 51, 59, 61, 103, 110, 111, 125
Southeast, 7, 32, 34, 36, 37, 58, 97, 125, 128, 192
Southern hospitality, 142, 147
Southern Jews, 105
Southern Professionals, 8
Southern writers, 187
Southernisms, 157, 159, 164, 165
Spoleto Festival, 51
STEM, 133
Stigall, John, 78

storytelling, 4, 8, 9, 186, 187, 188, 189, 190
Super Bowl, 125
Tennessee, 4, 5, 11, 12, 22, 28, 30, 32, 39, 40, 43, 53, 56, 59, 62, 67, 88, 89, 102, 105, 106, 109, 110, 111, 112, 118, 125, 129, 131, 159, 181, 191, 192
Tennessee Valley Authority and the Army Corps of Engineers, 59
Texas, 30, 32, 33, 50
The Citadel, 31
*The Commitments*, 122
The Masters, 126
The Nitty Gritty Dirt Band, 123
The Reverend Billie Dean, 91
The Swanee River, 121
The Trail of Tears, 37
The Virginia Company, 46, 47
Transplants, 8, 135, 139
Turner, Nat, 51
Twain, Mark, 85
Twain, Shania, 118
Underwood, Carrie, 118
Urban League, 76, 106, 191
Usher, 69, 122, 123
Virginia, 20, 25, 30, 46, 47, 48, 49, 51, 52, 111, 117, 121

196

Volkswagen Chattanooga, 9, 92, 131, 191, 193
Wagoner, Porter, 118
Walker, Alice, 186
Welty, Eudora, 186
West Virginia, 30, 111
Wolfe, Thomas, 187
Women's Council on Diversity, 138, 192
Wormser, Richard, 73
Wright, Richard, 186
Ziehres, Beate, 131
Zydeco, 96, 117

CPSIA information can be obtained at www.ICGtesting.com
Printed in the USA
LVOW05s1313030114

367819LV00012B/222/P

9 781489 553379